SHEEP-O

Sheep-O

A Collection of Stories from the Shearing World of Bygone Days

GURU "YORKY" OM

Oceaniacom Press

First published by Oceaniacom Press 2024
A division under Oceaniacom Pty Ltd.
www.oceaniacom.com

Sheep-O
Copyright © 2024 by Guru "Yorky" Om

ISBN (Print): 978-1-923113-04-6
ISBN (Ebook): 978-1-923113-05-3

All rights reserved. No part of this publication may be reproduced, stored in a retrieval system, or transmitted in any form or by any means without prior written permission from the publisher. This book is a nonfiction work based on real events and memoirs of the author. Every effort has been made to preserve the original voice of the author as closely as possible.

Edited by Sally-Anne Ward
Cover design by Alethea Van Holland

Oceaniacom Press supports copyright. Thank you for supporting copyright and buying an authorized copy from Oceaniacom Press, a division under Oceaniacom Pty Ltd. Your commitment to respecting the intellectual property of creators contributes to the world of literature and enter-tainment. We appreciate your dedication to fostering a culture that values and protects the works of imagination. Together, letÕs continue to celebrate and uphold the importance of creative expression. Visit us online at: www.oceaniacom.com for more literary adventures.

FOREWORD

In the tapestry of life's grand journey, few threads are woven with the vibrancy and resilience of Guru Om's spiritual odyssey. From the humble beginnings in the Midlands of the UK, his quest for truth transcended borders, leading him to the sacred lands of India and the diverse landscapes of Australia, New Zealand and the Americas. Unfettered by the transient opinions of the world, Guru Om emerged as a guiding light, illuminating the path for those who seek authenticity in their existence.

As both his agent and publisher, I am deeply honoured to preserve and disseminate the wisdom he has garnered, especially his observations on the peculiarities of Australian life. His reflections delve into the heart of our nation's unique institutions and our intricate relationship with the Indigenous Australians. It is my sincere hope that his profound insights resonate not only within the shores of Australia but also echo across the globe, reaching readers yearning to understand the essence of our collective human experience.

Guru Om's narrative is a testament to the unyielding spirit of inquiry and the boundless potential for growth when one is liberated from the weight of societal judgment. May his words serve as a beacon of truth, guiding you through the rich landscape of his experiences to the core of our shared reality.

Guy Perrine
CEO/Founder
Oceaniacom Press

"SHEEP-O"

Shouted out, is a term used when the shearer needs his pen filled up. That's the 'penner-uppers' job to make sure the shearer doesn't run out of sheep.

Speed means money!

| 1 |

First Attempt At Shearing

"You'd better have a good breakfast this morning 'cause after breakfast we're going up the paddock to bring the sheep in. I noticed the other day a few fly-blown wethers in 'em, so we'll have to shear 'em and stick a bit of tar on 'em."

"Oh great," I said. "I've only ever seen sheep-shearing on the telly in England. Maybe I can have a go at it, Burt?"

"Ya can have a go but it's the hardest job in Australia, mate. I doubt whether you'd even be able to git the belly wool off a' one.

"Can you shear Burt?" I said.

"Yeh, but I'm not real fast at it 'cause I don't get enough practice. You've gotta have a heart as big as a football and a brain the size of a split pea to make a good shearer."

After breakfast, me and Burt took off up the paddock with his two black-barb dogs to muster up the sheep. The sheep were scattered all over one of his Bush paddocks and it took the dogs quite a while to round up the rough, woolly wethers. Once the dogs had rounded up as many sheep as they could find, we started on our way back to the house-paddock where the shearing-shed stood. On the way back Burt's old dogs saw a mob of Roos and decided to chase them. Old Burt had a shitfit when the dogs ran off and left us to look after the mob of sheep.

"Come here, ya black bastards!" roared Burt. "Git over here ya useless fucking bastards!"

The dogs paid no attention to Burt, whatsoever, so we had to wait for them to come back before we could move on.

"That's what fucking happens when I let 'em go Roo hunting! The bastard's git lazy. They'd sooner chase Roos than work sheep!"

When the dogs got back, old Burt gave 'em a real good hiding with a stick.

"Look at the black bastards!" said Burt. "They're not worth a portion of urine now! They're rooted from chasing bloody Roos in the hot sun!"

The two dogs were now laid under a shady tree with their tongues hanging out, having a breather and catching a new breath.

"I'll shoot ya next time!" yelled Burt at his two dogs who still lay there, panting and heaving.

We waited in the shade of a Gum tree for a while. Then old Burt roared, "Alright you pair a' bastards, go back! Go back Rover, you black, lazy bastard! Fetch 'em up Darky, ya useless, stupid bastard! I could do a better job myself if I had a couple more legs!" Then, he turned, and had a piece of me, "And you, ya useless pommy bastard, don't just stand there lookin', open the fuckin' gate! What d'ya expect 'em to do, jump over?"

'Fuck you Burt!' I said under mi breath.

"What did you say?" he roared, as he came towards me.

"Nothing Burt." I said, as I ran for the gate.

"Open both sides!" he roared. "That's why there's two gates! You're as dumb as those two fuckin' dogs, ya pommy bastard!"

At long last and a lot of cursing later, the sheep were now in the yards When we got back to the house, old Burt was as cool-as-a-cucumber again.

Burt started the Briggs & Stratton motor. He pressed the governor down and swung the handle on the large fly wheel. The engine popped and backfired a few times, then spit out a cloud of blue smoke from the exhaust pipe and slowly came to life. After the engine was warmed up, Burt put the wide, long belt over the shiny pulley, which drove the long overhead shaft and the shearing shed rattled into life.

The rotten floorboards vibrated and the tin on the side of the shed shook as the engine cranked away. Burt now stood at one of the shearing stands. He stripped down to his pants and singlet and tied some string just below the knees of his thick ex-army pants for a bo-yang. Then he picked up one of the ancient hand-pieces which were aptly named 'hot boxes'. (Some shearers call them 'bog-eyes' because they resemble a bog-eyed lizard.) He put a 3-pronged cutter in place and after that he screwed a comb down on top, screwed down the tension knob, put a good squirt of black sump oil over the comb and cutter, then pushed the ferule on the down pipe and pulled the bog-eye into gear for a test run.

CLUNK! ZZZZZZZZZZZ. The counterweight swung over when Burt pulled the string and the hand-piece was now running. He screwed down the tension knob a couple more clicks before he was satisfied it would cut. He pulled it out of gear and said to me, "Go grab me a sheep, we'd best git started!"

I opened the pen gate which was held on by some fencing wire and went inside to grab one of the wethers. As soon as I tried to turn it over, the saffron thistles stuck in mi finger ends. I pulled my hand back quickly and removed the long thistle. "

"What's the matter with ya now?" said Burt. "The wool's full of thistles!"

"'Course it fuckin' is! They've been running in a thistle paddock for a couple of months. You'll get used to it in a few days. Anyways, how are ya gonna learn to shear 'em if ya can't stand a few burrs in ya hands!"

It took Burt about 10 minutes to shear the flyblown wether. As he was shearing it, I was thinkin' to myself; 'I could do that and I could probably do a better job than Burt. When I get off his place, one day I'm going to shear sheep for a living.'

After the sheep was shorn, old Burt straightened his black and then shoved the sheep out the porthole into the 'counting-out' pen. He showed me how to grab the fleece and throw it on the skirting table where Bill was waiting to skirt it.

"After you've thrown it on the table, sweep up the board and get me another sheep." said Burt.

When he had shorn about 15 sheep, I said to him, "Hey Burt, can I have a go at shearing?"

"Ya can finish this one off for me when I get on the last side."

As soon as Burt had shorn the sheep to the last shoulder just below the leg, he pulled the string and the bug-eye stopped running.

"Here ya go mate." he said as he handed me the hand-piece. "Ya stick him between ya legs like that, bend over him and push down hard on the shoulder with ya left hand. Start from there and run the hand-piece on the skin down to his flank. The next blow is supposed to start from here and run it down out to his toe and be careful not to hock him 'cause if ya hamstring him he's dog tucker! Are ya ready?"

"Ready!" I said.

The bog-eye hand-piece was red hot when old Burt handed it to me. I was determined not to complain. Burt pulled the string and the hand- piece flew into gear. The dirt in the wool had blunted the comb and cutter and the tension on the hand-piece was so tight it made it want to twist and spin out of mi hand. I put the comb on the skin and slowly pushed it forwards. The down-tube swung around and the comb dug into the skin as I pushed it down towards the flank.

"Keep it in the wool!" said Burt.

By now there was blue oil smoke bellowing out of the comb and cutter. "Keep it on the skin and cutting wool, then it will stay cool!" said Burt, as I struggled to control the bog-eye. The rough-looking wether had worked it out that this was my first go at shearing so just to make it interesting for me, he complicated matters worse than they already were by trying to kick my head off.

"Sit down, ya bastard!" I said, as I tried to keep the hot machine down on the skin but the sheep never took any notice, he kept right on kicking.

"Ya gotta keep the bottom tooth on the skin, mate, if ya wanna make a good, clean shearer!" Burt said.

It took me, at least, 10 minutes to finish off the wether. The sweat was now pouring out of me as I bent over him. When I eventually finished shearing him, he looked like a lawnmower had attacked him. There were nicks and cuts all over his back leg and pieces of half-cut wool stuck out all over him. My hand was burned to a blister from the hot bog-eye and my back already had a sharp, crampy pain just above mi bum.

"Is that good enough Burt?"

"Gawd struth mate! It looks as though ya plucked him! Give 'im to me and I'll clean him up for ya."

Burt took the sheep and the bog-eye from me and finished cleaning up the wrinkly, old wether. He pulled the string out of gear and the bog-eye stopped. Then he kicked the sheep down the chute and said to me, "Stop the engine. That'll do us for today. We'll make an early start on 'em tomorrow."

"That job is a lot harder than it looks!" I said to Burt.

"Sure is mate. I'm not much of a shearer but ya should see some of those blokes who live in town. There's one bloke - Johnny Burt.

He shore 250 one day out at Merri Merrigal. He's a real fair-dinkum gun shearer. The only problem is he likes his grog too much. They tell me, in town, that he shore over 200 a day for 2 weeks and at the end of the shed he was in debt to the contractor for 50 quid."

"What did he do with all that money?"

"He pissed it up against the wall, mate and blew the rest on the horses and cards."

"One day, I'm going to be a gun shearer."

"It takes a lot of balls to be a gun shearer and yours are no way big enough to take on that job yet."

"Don't you worry. One day I'll be twice as fast as you are."

| 2 |

Digging a Dunny Hole

Once all of Rogers' crop was sown down, I'd worked miself out of another job. Back to Lake Cargelligo I went. This time, I had to find a place to live so I went over to Twitchey's Hotel to enquire how much a room would cost on a residential basis which also made it cheaper. I was now in a position to hang around the bars. It wasn't that I liked hangin' around drunks but if I wanted to find casual work, all business was conducted from a bar stool in any one of the Lakes' three hotels. I had a few bucks tucked away now from all the long hours of tractor drivin'.

One Sunday morning I went into the bar to look for some work. Someone I knew introduced me to a real beaut young bloke called Kenny Carlton. We got on well together right from the word go.

"Where ya working, Yorky?" he asked.

"Nowhere yet, Kenny. I've just finished tractor driving out at Roger Tom's place."

"Why don't ya git a job roust-a-bouting in the shearing sheds?"

"I'd love that but I don't know how to go about it."

"It's easy, mate. I'll introduce ya to a few of the local contractors and ya can take it from there."

"How did you learn to shear, Mate?"

"Mi old man's a shearer, he taught me. I've been going out in the sheds with him since I was a kid."

"Is it hard work?"

"Well, it's not easy but once ya git the blows down and git fit, then it depends on how hard ya wanna' work."

"What's the money like?"

"If ya git in good sheep ya can make a good, few bob."

"What's the going rate?"

"Eighteen bucks a hundred."

"How many can you shear a day, Kenny."

"Oh about 120-130."

"Shit! That's big money." I said.

"Yeah," he said. "If ya can keep ya self in work it is."

I left the bar for a while to go for a feed. When I came back, Kenny was still sat on the same stool, a few middies worse for wear. Kenny was a short nuggety bloke, clean-cut and well-dressed. He had short, straight hair and a somewhat chubby face. His arms were quite big from dragging sheep. The knuckles on both his hands were swollen as most shearers' hands are. I noticed his arms were covered in scratches and burr marks from the saffron thistles that were all over the sheep's fleece.

When I walked over to him, he said in a somewhat slurred voice, "Ya see that bloke over the other side of the bar, Yorky?"

"Yeah."

"His name's Donny Freeman. Go and see him, mate. Tell him ya looking for a job roust-a- boutin'."

When I went over to where he was sitting, I waited for him to finish talking to his mate.

"G'day." I said.

"G'day mate, what can I do for ya?"

"I'm looking for some work in the sheds. Kenny Carlton said ya might have some."

"Kenny sent ya over, did he?"

"Yeah." I said.

"I haven't got anything going for a couple of days but I can give ya some work down at my house till we start, if ya like."

"That sounds great!"

"Hang on a minute till I finish mi beer." Don Freeman was a tall, lanky bloke. He had wavy hair, a gaunt face and a husky, muffled voice which came from a broken nose. He downed his 7 ounce and said, "What's ya name?"

"Yorky."

"A chummy, eh? Can ya work, mate? Ya don't look too fuckin' big to me!"

"Don't let the size fool ya." I said.

"Alright mate, let's go."

"Where we off to?" I asked, as we walked out of Twitchey's, down the main street towards the Lake.

"Down to my joint. It's just down at the end of the street."

When we got inside of his backyard he said, "I want to put a big septic tank over here so I need a hole digging. D'ya think ya can do that?"

"How big a hole d'ya want?"

"I'll show ya."

He walked over to a wheel barrow and took out a string line and two pegs. He stuck one peg in the ground and then unravelled the string. When the string was straight, he tied the steel peg on and then walked around with the peg scratching the hard ground as he went. Once the circle was complete, he said, "That's about nine foot across and it's gotta be seven foot deep. Ya think ya can dig it by hand?"

"No worries, mate."

"How long will it take ya?"

"Probably all day." I said.

"One day?" he said. "That's all? That's a fuckin' big hole mate! There's a lot of diggin' there!"

"Yeah! About one day's worth."

"Shit! I doubt whether an Aussie could dig that in two days, let alone a chummy in one!"

"One day, mate." I said.

"Alright chummy, the jobs yours! How much is it gonna cost me?"

"Tell ya what, Don. You don't think I can do it in one day and ya said it would take an Aussie two days. At a dollar an hour, that's 16 bucks for two eight-hour days. I'll make ya a deal. If you promise to give me a job as a roust-a-bout as soon as you've got work, I'll dig the hole for ten bucks and I'll finish it within the day."

"You're on chummy!" he said with a smile. "Ya can start in the sheds with me on Wednesday, that's if ya finish the septic hole in time. I won't be here tomorrow so I'll leave the pick, shovel and the crowbar in that wheelbarrow over there. Alright chummy?"

"Alright Donny." I said, with a big smile. "Be careful ya don't fall in it if ya come home full!" I joked.

"I'll believe it when I see it!"

I was up the next morning, bright and early. I had a bit of breakfast at the Hotel before I set off. As I walked down the empty street towards Don's place, I was thinking what it would be like to work in the shearing sheds. I'd always wanted to learn shearing ever since I had a go at it at old Burt's place. When I walked through the small gate and down the dirt path, I decided to put everything out of my mind except the big job that was ahead of me. It was still pretty cool as the sun was not yet above the horizon. I stood in the rough, untidy side-yard contemplating what was the best and easiest way to go about diggin' the septic tank hole.

After a few minutes it became obvious to me that there was no easy way to dig it. The only way it was going to get done was to start digging!

"G'day." said Donny as he peered down into the hole. "Grand streuth chummy, ya finished it mate!"

"Right on seven feet!" I said as I looked up at him from down in the hole.

"You're a bloody little beauty chummy! I didn't think ya stood a mongrel dog's chance in hell of finishing that today!"

"I told ya I could do it. Good-looking hole, mate, eh?"

"Not bad chummy. It's a pity we're gonna fill it with shit! How ya gonna git out 'a the hole?" he said, with a big grin.

"Give us a pull up mate or I'll be here all night."

Once I got out of the hole, I said to him, "So I've got a job in the sheds with ya now, mate?"

"Tell ya what, Chummy, ya can work in the sheds with me anytime I've got work. Any man who can dig a hole that big and deep in one day is good enough for me, sport. You're a better man than most of those lazy bastards that sit around the bar all day. They ask me for a job and I take 'em out and they're too crook from the grog to do any good!"

"Will ya teach me to shear, mate?"

"If I get time I will and if not one of the other blokes will!"

Although I was knackered from the day's work, the thought of working in the sheds and learning to shear put a shit-eating grin on my face for the rest of the evening. A couple of days later I saw Don in Twitchey's bar.

"Ya got a start tomorrow if ya want it, chummy!"

" 'Course I want it! What time will ya pick me up?"

"Be ready at six. I'll pick ya up on mi way past."

"How many days will ya have for me?"

"Two days this week then we'll start on a new shed next week. It should go for three weeks."

| 3 |

Into the Shearing Shed

I was sat on the curb outside Twitchey's at quarter to six, in the morning, waiting for the contractor. As I sat there wondering what shed life would be like, a car horn beeped and Don Freeman pulled into the curb.

"G'day Don."

"G'day Chummy. Hop in mate, we've gotta pick up the other blokes."

As I got in the front of the Falcon Sedan he said, "I hope Gundy's sober this morning. He was pissed as a chook yesterday. It took him a couple of hours to sober up. He only shore 15 sheep the first run."

"Isn't 15 sheep a lot to shear in one run?" I asked.

"That's nothin' for a shearer of Gundy's capabilities, Chummy. When Gundy's sober and he feels like workin', I've seen him shear a couple of hundred in a day and not break out in a sweat. 'Course he's very rarely sober!"

We drove around Chaman's corner where all the black fellas hang out. There was a couple of them sitting on a bench, swigging on a half- gallon flagon of plonk.

"I don't know how those blokes do it!" said Don. "I've seen 'em sat there in the hot sun all day getting' full on plonk."

"Where do they git the money from?" I asked.

"They get a government check every week. Most of 'em spend the whole lot on cheap plonk."

We pulled into the curb again and a young bloke, about my age, hopped in the front beside me.

"G'day Freeman, how ya going mate?" he said.

"G'day Boney. D'ya know chummy?"

"I've heard of ya mate. Mi brother Kenny told me about ya."

"Good to meet ya Boney." I said as we shook hands.

"How's Kenny doing?" asked Don.

Boney, who was a small, thin bloke with jet-black hair and a cheeky smile, said with a laugh, "He's fast asleep in the front seat of his car. He got full as a boot again last night. He drove home from Twitchey's but he was too drunk to make it from the car to our front door."

"How long till she has the kid?" asked Donny.

"About a month, I think. I asked Kenny the same question and he said, 'what kid?'" Boney had a real good laugh over this little joke.

"This is gonna be Chummy's first day in the shed Boney so teach him all the ropes, eh mate."

"Ya haven't worked in the sheds before Chummy?"

"Only for half-a-day at old Burt Booth's place."

"They tell me old Burt's a bit of a hard man to work with." said Donny.

"That's an understatement!" I said.

Everyone had a good laugh at that. Shearers and roust-a-bouts are always trying to take the piss out of each other, probably 'cause it makes the day go by easier and relieves the tension from the hard work.

The car pulled up in front of a weatherboard house and Donny Freeman honked on the horn. After a few minutes a bloke appeared at the door and called out, "Be right with ya!"

"Jeezus!" said Don. "Old Gundy doesn't look too good to me this morning. I heard he was as full as a boot up at Giltraps bar last night."

"He doesn't mind a drop now and then." said Boney with a giggle.

"Ya not wrong there. It's a bit hard to say anything about it 'cause he's such a good shearer. Even when he's crook from the grog he's cleaner and faster than a lot of blokes."

The front door of Gundy's house opened and Gundy walked out. He looked a bit sick and unsteady on his feet as he walked over the dead, patchy grass of his front lawn. Just before he got to the car, his old lady came running after him with a packet of fags in her hand. He took the fags from her and never said a word.

As Gundy reached the back door of the car, he tripped over a crack in the cement and nearly crashed into the window.

"Open the back door for him Chummy before he hurts himself." said Don.

Leaning mi arm over the back seat, I pulled up on the handle and pushed on the door. The door almost knocked Gundy over and he took a couple of steps backwards.

Very carefully, he maneuvered round the open door and slowly got in the back of the Sedan.

"Ya tryin' to knock me arse over head?" said Gundy as he made himself comfortable.

"No, it was my fault for shoving the door so hard." I said.

"What's your name?" "Yorky."

"What kinda fucking name is that?" he said, with slurred speech.

"It's a nickname, 'cause I come from Yorkshire."

"Fucking hell!" said Gundy.

"A pommy fucking bastard! What ya doin' in the sheds?"

"It's Chummy's first day. We're gonna teach him to roust-a-bout." said Don.

"Chummy eh! That's not a bad fuckin' name. I think I'll call ya Chummy from now on."

"Did ya have a hard night at Giltrap's, Gundy?" asked Boney.

"I sure fuckin' did mate. I never got home till 1 o'clock this morning and the missus was as cranky as hell with me. She made me sleep on the couch all night. She was still cranky when she woke me up this morning. Oh shit, mi head's not too good either. Hey Freeman."

"What d'ya want Gundy?"

"Can ya go a bit easier on those fuckin' corner mate? Mi brain's sloshing around in last night's grog!"

"How many are ya gonna shear today, if I slow down?" said Don in a joking way.

"How many did I shear yesterday?"

"A hundred and two."

"Alright, I'll shear 140 today. How's that?"

"Could you do 150, please?" said Don, taking the piss out of Gundy.

"You fuckin' contractors are never satisfied?" said Gundy, as he pulled a fag out of his packet.

"Give us a light Boney."

"I haven't got one Gundy."

"Here ya go Gundy." I said as I flicked the lighter.

"Good on ya Chummy, ya pommy bastard. Me and you are gonna git on real well mate!"

Gundy was a very funny character. He was about 5'10" with dry, wavy hair. He had a bald spot in the middle of his head and the hair was starting to thin at the front. His eyes were blue and his broken nose shot off to the side at a very acute angle. He was dressed in the usual shearer's garb which was a cardigan, blue singlet with a reinforced patch on the left front side, double-legged, heavy duty blue denim shearers dungarees which helped, slightly, to keep the thistles out, woolly socks and shearers boots. The trousers were held up with an elastic belt made out of good-quality surgical elastic.

"Where's that fuckin' Athel Cook this morning, Freeman?" asked Gundy.

"We're gonna pick him up now. Suppose he was with ya at Giltrap's last night, was he?"

"Yeah. The bastard tried to miss out on buying a round before he left. He can be as tight as a fishes arse sometimes."

The car ground to a halt at the far-end of town and another shearer was sat on the curb, smoking a home-made. He was a thick-set bloke with a whiskery face. Not a very good-looking bloke at all. His thick, wavy hair was plastered down on his large head and he had a sweat towel around his neck like a scarf.

"G'day, ya fuckin' bastards." he said as he got in the back beside Gundy.

"G'day." said Don. "This is Chummy, Athel.

He's roust-a-boutin' for us today."

"G'day Athel." I said as I leaned over to shake his hand.

"A fucking pommy bastard eh? I've never seen a good one yet!"

"'This one's a fucking beaut, so go easy on him today Athel. It's his first day."

Don let the clutch out and the Sedan sped off out of town onto the dirt road heading for the Cocky's shearing shed.

"Have ya ever had ya balls tarred Chummy?" asked Athel as were were driving along.

"No! Why d'ya ask?"

"'Cause that's what we do with first-time rousies!"

"Not this time Athel." said Don. "I told ya already, leave him alone mate!"

Athel Cook was not a pleasant character. He seemed to take an instant dislike to me. As we were driving along, Boney leaned across and whispered, "Take no notice of Athel. He's a fucking yobbo."

He must have had quite good ears 'cause he said to Boney, "What's that ya fuckin' say Boney?"

"Nothing mate." said Boney with a giggle.

Athel leaned over and twisted Boney's ear and Boney, small as he was, got really pissed at him.

"Keep ya fuckin' hands to ya self Athel or I'll fuckin' job ya one mate!"

"You and whose fucking army?" said Athel. "Just try it again, ya fuckin' yobbo and I'll show ya!"

"Come on you blokes," said Freeman. "Ya worse than a pack of mongrel shed dogs!"

"Yeah, that's right. You tell 'em Freeman." said Gundy.

"Give us another light Chummy." he said with a twisted grin.

The rest of the drive to the shed was done in silence as we sped along the dirt track road at 70 miles an hour. Half an hour later we pulled off the main Rankin Springs Road and turned into the Cocky's property. Boney jumped out and opened the gate, once it was closed again, we drove up a narrow, winding bush track and stopped in front of a big, old, somewhat dilapidated shearing shed. There were another two shearers' cars parked out front and the yards were chock-a-block full of unshorn sheep.

When we got inside the shed Don introduced me to all the other shearers and rousies and Boney filled me in on the 'board-boys' job. Gundy was a really fair-dinkum bloke, even though he was a chronic drunk. I stood around and talked and joked with him as we waited for the bell to ring at 7:30.

In a four-stand shearing shed there are usually 4 shearers and one board-boy, a wool-classer, a rousie to help skirt the fleeces, a wool-presser whose job it is to press the wool into large bales and sometimes a 'penner-uppa'. His job is to keep the shed pens full. The contractor's job is to grind up the combs and cutters, count the sheep out of each shearers outside the pen at the end of the run, which is 2 hours and make sure everything runs smoothly between the shed- hands and the farm-hands.

"Will ya teach me to shear, Gundy?" I asked. "Oh, I might do Chummy. Let's see how you go at roust-a-boutin' first mate. Maybe you won't like the shearing sheds!"

"I already like 'em and when I can shear, I'll be working for miself. That's what I want to do."

"Alright Chummy. Look out mate, the bells about to go!"

The bell rang right on 7:30. All the 4 shearers went through the pen gate to grab their first sheep. Gundy was the last to finish and when he let his sheep go down the chute, he straightened up and I noticed the look of pain on his face.

"Jeezus, Chummy, it's going to be another hard day for me." he said.

The board-boys job, which I was doing, could be pretty hard at times. I had to pick up the fleeces from 4 shearers and keep the shearing board swept clean of dag's and loose pieces of wool.

At the end of my first day, I was pretty tired of running about so much but I knew, more than ever, I was going to learn shearing no matter what it took. The shearers were always in a good mood on the way home from the sheds. The They laughed and joked about the day's work and talked about the first cold beer they were going to have at Giltrap's Hotel when we hit town. Giltrap's was commonly known around town as the Blood House. It got its name from the amount of fights that took place in the bar. The fights at Giltrap's were usually conducted by the Abos or in a lot of cases, a feud between the white fellas and the black fellas.

There were many stories floating around town about those brawls. A lot of the local people were not too keen on drinking at Giltrap's in case they got sucked into one of the evenings fights.

"Isn't Giltrap's a rough house Gundy?" I asked as we walked up the front steps.

"She sure is Chummy but it's not as boring as those as those other two fuckin' places mate." Giltrap's was packed as we entered.

"Who's buying the first round?" said Gundy, as we pushed our way to the bar.

"The first one's are on me." said Don Freeman.

"What'll you have men?" Once the orders were taken by Don, he called Giltrap over, who was busy drinking in three different schools.

"What'll ya have Freeman?" asked Giltrap. Don gave the order, including a 5-ounce beer for me.

"How old's the young bloke?" said Giltrap as he looked at me.

"Oh, that's Chummy." said Don.

"He's old enough. He's working out in the sheds with me now."

"Whatever you say Freeman but if he isn't and the old Sarg comes in, tell him to hide his beer or I'll git in the shit!"

Drinking grog was a part of the shearer's world. It seemed to go with the job. Shearers lose gallons of sweat every day so they put it back in, of an evening, as fast as they can. We all sat or stood around for the next three hours bull-shitting and making jokes, taking the piss out of each other and generally having a good old time.

| 4 |

The One Tree Plain

On Friday night, after the shed had finished, Don Freeman said to me, "We're starting a campin'-out shed on Monday Chummy, so we'll be leaving the lake on Sunday, lunchtime. Make sure you've got enough gear for the week, including booze and fags 'cause we'll be way out in the bush, miles from nowhere."

"Where we going Don?"

"Down towards Hay, on the One Tree Plain. I contract that shed every year. We'll be there for roughly three weeks mate."

"OK mate, I'll be ready."

That evening, being Friday night and the end of a shed, Gundy was firing on all 8 cylinders already.

"Hey Chummy!" Gundy yelled. "Come over and meet Cyclone. This is our pommy roust-a-bout." said Gundy to Cyclone.

"This is Cyclone, Chummy. He's a gun shearer!"

Cyclone was as bad, if not worse an alcoholic than Gundy. Once he had a few bucks in his pocket he would not shear another sheep until it was all gone. Cyclone, like Gundy, was a hell of a good-natured man but the booze had him. He was his own worst enemy. Very seldom, in the Bush, will one man tell another man what he should do. Everyone figures that as soon as a boy starts to work, he's old enough to be his own master, 'cause for one thing, he's working and living in a man's world.

When Sunday lunchtime arrived, Don Freeman picked up Boney and me, Gundy and Cyclone. We drove a long way down to the One Tree Plain. Boney and I had to sit in the back of the Ute 'cause there was no room in the front. The back of the Ute was filled with stores for the cook. A section of the back was reserved for me and Boney, along with the cartons of beer and numerous flagons of Brown Muscatel wine. Freeman's dogs had to balance on top of all the boxes. They almost fell out a couple of times as we sped along the Bush roads at 80 miles an hour.

After a few hours of driving, we arrived at the shearing shed. There it was, a big, corrugated iron shed sat on wooden pylons out in the middle of nowhere! The landscape was almost barren as far as the eye could see in all directions. The ground was hot and dry. Every so often there was a clump of rough, dry bush grass.

It was called the One Tree Plain because nowhere in sight could anyone point out a tree of any size or shape. It was so hot that numerous whirly winds chased each other round and round in circles as they sped across the barren land. There was nothing edible that Merino sheep could live on and how they survived got me beat! The yards were already full of big, rough-necked wethers and a few hundred were packed in under the shed in case of a freak rainstorm. Miles and miles off in the distance was a cloud of red dust. This was probably the Jackeroos mustering another large mob of sheep. It would take a full day to bring them in to the shed to wait for their turn for shearing.

The shearers living quarters were about a hundred yards away from the shed so Freeman drove the Ute in that direction. There was no shade to park it in so it just stayed where it was stopped until it had been unloaded. Most shearers quarters at camp-out sheds are pretty clean and have good mattresses and beds. The beds, are in most cases, two to a room. Boney and me picked a clean room at the end, before any of the other blokes arrived. The Shearers Union, which is called the A.W.U. was very supportive towards the shearers. That's the reason the quarters were in such good shape. If it was left up to the Cocky, he wouldn't care if the shearer had to sleep on the floorboards because, by his reckoning, the quarters were only used once or twice a year at shearing and crutching time, so why bother to make them liveable. Each room had a small set of cupboards between the beds for our clothes. The one window had a fly screen to keep out the bush flies and mosquitoes. There were no fans to keep it cool and at night- time it could be around 90 degrees in those tin rooms. There was no electricity so the two refrigerators in the kitchen ran on kerosene. Half of one fridge would be used to keep the beer cold and the rest of the grog would be wrapped in wet hessian bags and stuck under the floor outside. Whatever bit of breeze there was would keep the beer slightly cool but nowhere near cold. Boney and I helped Don to cart the stores from the back of the Ute to the kitchen.

After we'd finished, Boney said, "Come on Chummy, let's go over to the shearing shed and check it out mate!"

It was about 5 o'clock now and the heat was still stifling. Mirages of water appeared everywhere as we walked across the windy plain. The hot breeze made doing anything hard work so we took our time, laughing and joking as we walked. We got to the big shed and walked up the steep wooden stairs, hanging onto the steel railing. I was in front, so I pushed open the small corrugated door and we went inside.

"Gaw'd fucking hell!" said Boney as we stood in the shed and looked around. "Just look at all that parrot shit on the floor! It'll take us two or three hours to clean up this mess!"

"Yeah. Just look up there Boney!"

The shearing shed rafters were packed tight with Galahs. As we walked around, I said to Boney, "Why are they all hanging around in the shed, mate?"

"'Cause there's no fucking trees around Chummy so they've taken over the shearing shed."

The shed had been closed for months on end so due to the heat inside, there were layers of parrot shit all over the place. The stink was awful.

"Fuckin' hell Chummy, we've got to get rid of these bloody Galahs and clean up this board before we can even start shearin'."

"Yeah, it's a real mess Boney. How d'ya reckon we should go about it?"

"We'll kill as many of 'em as we can because if not, they'll come back at night-time and shit all over the place again."

"How we gonna' do that mate? If we shoot at 'em and miss, the bullets will put holes in the roof."

"Ya probably right Chummy. Give me a minute to think, mate."

There must have been at least 300 Galahs in the shed. Some were sitting while others were flying around and squawking like hell. As I looked around, there was shit on the floor, shit on the wool table, all over the wool press, the wool packs were covered in it and it was even in the wool stalls.

"Tell ya what we'll do Chummy. Let's take that full bale of wool and roll it over to that end of the shed."

After that was done, Boney said, "Alright mate, grab that end of the wool table and we'll carry it over to the opposite side."

As soon as the table was in place, he said, "Here Chummy, take this."

"What's the straw broom for?"

"It's not a fuckin' straw broom!" he said with a big grin on his face.

"It looks like a straw broom to me, mate."

"Use your imagination Chummy. It's a double-handed shuttle-cock racquet!"

"Where's the shuttle-cocks?"

"Up there stupid!" as he pointed to the Galahs.

"Now, I've got the picture mate! I'll use the table and you use the bale."

"That's the idea Chummy. You scare 'em down to my end for a while and I'll smash 'em with the broom. We'll take turns at batting. Let's see who can get the highest number." He drew a line in the parrot shit and said, "That's your half and this is mine. We'll count up later."

I shooed all the Galahs down to Boney's end of the shed and as they approached him, he swung the straw broom with a double back- hander. 'WHACK!' He knocked three Galahs out of the air in one blow. A double-handed forearm smash sent two more crashing to the floor.

"Alright Chummy, your turn," he said as he giggled out loud. "I'll shoo 'em down to your end now mate. You take a couple of serves. The double-handed forearm smash seems to be a good point-scorer!"

As I stood on the table at the ready, the long- handled straw broom was over mi shoulder, cocked and ready to serve.

"Here they come Chummy!" yelled Boney.

Three hundred Galahs were now squawking like hell and flying straight for me. As soon as the live shuttle-cocks were in range, I let fly with a powerful over-head serve! One large Galah was knocked out of the air. An unconventional, two- handed upward reverse stroke sent two more to the deck. A clumsy double-handed sideswipe sent three more crashing through the ether!

"OK, your serve Boney!" I yelled, amidst the loud squawking. I shooed the Galahs back down to Boney's court. A well-aimed side-swipe sent three Galahs to bird heaven. A single-handed clumsy shot missed altogether and Boney fell off the big wood bale into a pile of Galah shit.

"Fault!" I shouted from my end as he slipped around in the white shit trying to scramble back up on the 'baseline' pack. Another mighty double-handed backhand sent three more Galahs to the deck.

"Alright Chummy, your serve!" yelled Boney as he shooed them back again.

After half-an-hour of strenuous badminton on centre court we called 'Time-Out' for a rest and clean-up. It wasn't too bad but Boney was covered in Galah shit and feathers as he walked up to me, smiling from ear to ear.

"We'll take a breather and swap ends Chummy. That wool pack is a bit hard to balance on. You've got the advantage on the table."

"Alright mate." I said as we laughed.

"We'll swap ends and play one more game and then we'll open the doors and chase the rest out. I don't think they'll come back in a hurry."

At the end of the game, we counted up the Galahs and then opened the two large doors. The remaining parrots flew out and were never seen again. It took Boney and me three hours to scrub the floor with hot, soapy water we'd boiled in the outside copper. By this time all the other blokes had arrived. The cook made up some tucker and after dinner we sat around in our rooms reading, talking or playing cards. Gundy and a couple of the other shearers sat around drinking plonk til about 11 o'clock.

It was pretty hard to sleep that night 'cause it was so hot. We just lay on our backs sweating like hell, drifting in an out of sleep. The following morning being Monday, everyone was up bright and early. Even Gundy didn't look too worse for wear. Breakfast was at 6 and Don's brother Jazzer was doing the cooking. Jazzer was a few years younger than Don, which would have made him around

40. Don was a fairly handsome sort of bloke which was more than could be said for Jazzer! He was about 5'9" and a thick-set bloke. Most of his bulk was comprised of fat. He had a mop of black, curly hair and a pretty large beak for a nose and a ginormous set of choppers on him. His teeth would not have looked too bad had he have cultivated the habit of cleaning them. Instead, they were a greeny-yellow color. He had a habit of standing with his mouth open and the teeth could easily be seen protruding below his top lip. He was also quite a heavy smoker. He used to grip the end of the tips in his large teeth. Have you ever seen a horse with its' lips peeled back as it chomps on the bit? Well, stick a fag in-between the horse's teeth and there you have Jazzer! As far as his cooking skills went, he was rated at half-a-star. Jazzer was also able to shear.

After breakfast, we all made our way over to the shearing shed. As we entered the shed Gundy noticed a large pile of dead Galahs off to the side of the steps. When Boney related the game of Badminton, Gundy had to smile which was unusual for him at 6:45 in the morning.

Wool packs were put in place and the catching pens were filled up. Six pieces of paper with the numbers 1 to 6 were folded up and put in a hat. After they'd been shook up, each shearer drew out a number which denoted which stand he would work on. Whoever drew number 1 was expected to do the reps job which meant, in the event of a problem arising, the representative had to speak for the men. He would complain to Freeman, who was the contractor and in turn Freeman would go and see the cocky. There are strict working rules governing a shearing team. The shearers all picked up their hand-pieces after the draw and then proceeded to screw a comb and cutter in place. At the back of the hand-piece was a screw hole which had to be filled with oil at the end of every run, which lasted 2 hours. Everything was now in place so everyone stood around waiting for the bell to go at 7:30.

When 7:30 arrived Freeman rang the bell. All six shearers entered their pens and grabbed hold of a big rough wether. After tipping it over on its arse they dragged it backwards by its front legs to the down tube where their stand was. Gundy sat up his sheep right front leg under the side of his ribs, tucked the other front leg behind his left elbow and pulled the string which set the shearing machine in motion. He adjusted the tension knob, then made 5 or 6 blows from the sheep's brisket down to its flank. He grabbed the now loose belly wool and threw it on the board. It was my job to pick 'em all up. Next, he ran the machine out the top of the back leg which trimmed all the wool off.

Turning the machine around, he made one long blow around the sheep's crutch from toe to toe. Then he shore the back leg. As soon as this was done he knocked the wool off the sheep's head, which is called a top knot. Taking a step forwards, the sheep was now at a slight angle between his legs as he bent over and opened up the neck wool. The machine disappeared under the wool until Gundy flicked his wrist and the machine re-appeared. He then proceeded to run his blows up the side of the wrinkly neck until it was clean. Picking up the front leg with his left hand, he ran the blows down it as he turned around. Once the leg was clean, he dropped the big wether on its back and started the long blow. In no time at all the sheep was half shorn. As Gundy dragged his right foot forwards he cleaned up round the horns and head.

After this was done, he pushed his blows over the wrinkles and down to the brisket. Then he cleaned around the shoulder and picked up the last front leg. In a matter of seconds, the leg was clean and he pushed he hand piece down to the last flank letting the sheep's head come forwards.

Woosh, woosh, woosh went the blows as Gundy's arm pushed the bogeye flat on the skin, out to the toe and then cleaned up over the tail.

"Clunk!" Gundy pulled the string again. The machine came out of gear. The sheep which was now shorn clean as a whistle fell through his legs and he pushed it down the shute with the sole of his right boot. Straightening up, he wiped the sweat from his brow and walked into the pen for another big, woolly wether.

A roust-a-bout listens for the clunking sound which the overhead gear makes when the shearer pulls the string. This means someone has just started or just finished a sheep. It can be a very demanding job, picking up the wool for 6 fast shearers. At 9:27 the bell goes and the shearer's is not allowed to go in the pen for another sheep until 10 o'clock. From 9:30 till 10 is Smoko. Half an hour to have a cup of tea and a sandwich. After that the shearer rolls a smoke and then cleans up the combs and cutters he's used, ready for grinding again. With about 10 minutes left before 10 o'clock, he lays on his back on the shearing board and puts his legs up on the wall. This little trick helps relieve the pain in his back from 2 hours of bending over, working his guts out.

At 10 o'clock the bell rings and the process is started all over again. By the time 5:30 rolls around it's no wonder the shearer likes a few beers. He has just finished slaving his guts out for 8 solid hours in heat that can reach 105- degree mark. Cyclone did the first few days shearing really hard. Each time he straightened up from shearing a sheep, the pain on his face and in his eyes could be felt by all. He must have been sat in Giltrap's bar for at least 3 weeks boozing all his money away. Many people didn't believe he could even shear a sheep, let alone be a gun shearer.

Each day, as he persevered with the task of getting fitter, his shearing and tally improved slowly but surely. By the end of the shed, old Cyclone was the top tally man. He was, as I said, a goodhearted man and never abused the rousie if a fleece was missed and left laying on his stand.

One evening, when Gundy and Cyclone were grogging on, they ran out of beer and plonk. Gundy said to me, "Hey Chummy, ya got any plonk left mate?"

"Sure do Gundy. Why?"

"Can we have some of it?" he said with a boyish grin.

"Tell ya what I'll do Gundy. You teach me to shear and I'll provide ya with a gallon of plonk and a carton of fags a week. How's that sound mate?"

"You're on Chummy. Now, go and fetch ya half-gallon flagon. We'll start ya payments off tonight!"

That evening Gundy and Cyclone almost finished the whole flagon off. I said to Gundy, "Fuckin' hell Gundy, you're like a big kid with a bag of lollies. Ya can't stop til you've drunk the lot!"

This little joke of mine sent old Gundy into fits of laughter along with a spasm of coughing. The following morning, true to his word, Gundy started my shearing lessons.

"Chummy, git over here mate, if ya wanna learn to shear."

I was down that board before the words had left his mouth. He pulled the machine out of gear and said, "Alright Chummy, ya can finish the last side. Pull his head forwards and put ya knees there. Now push down on his shoulder and hang onto the hand-piece."

The hand-piece was really hot from all the sand in the wool. It wanted to spin out of my hand as I tried to control it.

"Ya gotta keep it on the skin Chummy. It's the shortest way around the sheep mate. Run those blows straight down and out to the toe. Don't do any of that jabbing mate or it will become a habit."

The wool was actually coming off the skin as I pushed the hand-piece along the contours of the sheep.

"That's it Chummy. Keep the comb full and go slow until you've got all the blows down."

As I was finishing off the big wether, Athel Cook came walking up the board.

"What are you doing with that sheep Chummy, trying to root it mate?"

"I'm learning to shear Athel." I said without raising my head.

"You shear, ya pommy bastard, you'll never make a shearer as long as ya arsehole points to the ground mate!"

"He'll make a better shearer than you Athel." said Gundy.

"Bullshit mate. No fucking pommy will out- shear me Gundy."

"Tell ya what Athel," said Gundy. "I'll bet you, before this shed's over, that Chummy can shear a ewe in under 5 minutes!"

"Fuckin' bullshit Gundy." said Athel.

"I'll bet you 10 bucks and a gallon flagon of plonk mate."

"Alright Gundy, ya fucking on mate!"

As I pulled the machine out of gear, the sweat was pouring out of mi forehead and the small of mi back had a cramped pain in it from bending right over.

"Alright Chummy, ya heard that mate. I'm gonna make a good shearer out of you, just listen to what I tell ya and every spare moment ya have, stand in front of me and watch." said Gundy.

"Alright Gundy, I'll give it mi best shot mate. I won't let ya down."

Each day I started and finished off sheep for Gundy. Towards the end of the first week, I shore a wether from start to finish. It took me about 14 minutes and by the time I finished, I was drenched in sweat.

"Good on ya Chummy." said Gundy. "That wasn't too bad for a learner. We've got to work on the blows and keeping the machine flat on the skin."

| 5 |

The Eating Contest

One evening, at dinner time, I asked Jazzer the cook if there was any more dinner. I had been working really hard and my appetite was growing.

"There's plenty left in the kitchen, Chummy. Help ya self mate."

I filled my plate as full again as the first round. When I got back into the dining room everyone joked about the amount of food on the plate. Big Roy James, the presser, said, "I think I'll have another plateful myself."

He came back into the dining room with a huge amount of food on his plate. Freeman said to me, as a joke, "Hey Chummy, ya think ya can eat more than big Roy can?"

Just for the fun of it, I said, "'Course I can. Any day! Why?"

Gundy said to Freeman, "Here's 5 bucks that says he can!"

Freeman said, "Here's 5 bucks that says he can't!"

The other shearers and shed hands all placed their bets and the eating contest began. Roy and I took our places at opposite ends of the table. We stared at each other for a couple of seconds then started to eat our platefuls. Gundy gave a running commentary as we ate. Speed was not a factor; volume was what bets were based on. Roy and I finished off our second plate of food; mashed potatoes, cabbage, carrots, mutton and gravy.

After the third plateful we ran out of the main course. Then we started on the sweets! We ate a large bowl full of Apple Strudel each and then the bowls were filled up, ready to go again.

Halfway through the second bowl, big Roy said, "Fuck this for a joke! The pommy bastard's too good for me! He must have hollow, fuckin' legs."

"Come on Chummy, you've gotta finish that bowl to win!" said Gundy.

Very slowly, I finished off the bowl of Apple Strudel and then sat back in mi chair and relaxed. The winners of the contest collected their bets and then cheered.

"Are you full yet, Chummy?" asked Gundy.

As I sat there, I began to think, 'I don't want to have to do this again so I'd better seal up my win a bit safer.'

"Not really Gundy. I could eat a big, tasty bowl of cornflakes with milk and sugar."

No one believed I could eat another morsel so the bets were all on again. Freeman filled up a large bowl of cornflakes. I sat there and loosened mi belt. After stretching mi arms over the back of mi head, I slowly started on the cornflakes! The going was much slower now since big Roy had dropped out of the contest. 15 minutes later the bowl was clean! The winnings were all collected and Gundy was all smiles as he helped me to my room. Strangely enough, I slept quite well that night and the following day it was like it never happened.

| 6 |

Roy James' Earlobe

It was Friday night and there was only a week left before we cut out. Seeing as we had run out of plunk and tinnies, it was decided we'd knock off at 5 and make a run into Lake Cargelligo.

Roy James, who I'd won the food eating contest from was a big, rough bloke who no one put shit on. He was about 6 foot 2 and weighed about 250 pounds, with not an ounce of fat anywhere on his body. Roy was a good bloke who had a big heart although he was not overburdened with brains. His hair was swept straight back and covered in lanolin from picking up big armfuls of wool. He had a big cauliflower ear and a nose that had been broken too numerous a-times to remember. His good ear had a lobe missing. The jagged line that was left resembled a half-moon shape. He usually wore a blue singlet, stubby shorts and a pair of elastic-sided McWilliams riding boots, the flat-heeled type.

As the evening progressed and everyone got drunker, I found myself wondering what had happened to Roy's ear. So, in a lull in the conversation I said to Roy, "Hey Roy, what happened to your ear lobe mate?"

A few people standing around must have heard me ask the question because the bar suddenly went very quiet. Roy casually downed his beer, the glass not too visible in his huge, calloused hand.

"What did you say Chummy?" he said. He sort of turned sideways to glare at me.

"I was just wondering what happened to ya ear lobe Roy."

As he stared down at me, he said, "I've killed bigger men than you for asking much less than that."

"Alright Roy, I didn't mean to be disrespectful to ya but what did happen to your earlobe?"

"I was in a fight at the hotel in Bourke. A little bloke was taking the piss out of me and as we struggled on the barroom floor, he bit the end off mi ear and then spat it out!"

"Why didn't ya git it sewn back on?" I said with great interest.

"'Cause when the bloke spat it out on the floor, the publican's Jack Russell ran over and grabbed it and swallowed it."

"Fuckin' hell Roy, did that hurt?"

"I was too drunk to feel a thing but I felt it next morning after I'd sobered up! Who's round is it?" he said as the tension in the room started to dissipate.

Roy walked out to go to the toilet and while he was out, Freeman said, "I never knew that's what happened to his ear."

Gundy said, "You've got more guts than anyone else in this barroom Chummy. There isn't a man alive in Lake Cargelligo who's had the balls to ask Big Roy about his ear and he's been coming to the lake each shearing season for years now."

Everyone started to laugh as they joked with me.

"It's not that I've got guts," I said to Gundy, "I knew there must have been quite a story behind his ear 'cause it caught my attention so much so that I couldn't help but ask."

George Giltrap came around the bar to where we were all in a group and he said to me, "Here Chummy, have a middy. It's on the house mate. That's the best bit a fun I've had for ages."

The bar erupted in raucous laughter but as soon as Roy entered the room everything settled down to its normal volume. By the end of the evening everyone was well and truly full. The shearing shed on the One Tree Plain was now on its last day. I had shorn my first ewe in 4 minutes and 50 seconds. Gundy and the others had won their bet. Athel Cook was not too pleased about this.

That evening, in the bar room, he tried to make things hard for me by calling me a pommy bastard all evening. 15 years later, I was shearing around the Lake again. Athel, who was now about 60, had the misfortune of meeting me in Giltrap's. A bloke, Mark Hargraves, had been kind enough to find me some work. Athel would be working alongside of me for two weeks.

On Sunday night, he was trying his best to upset me by calling me derogatory names and telling everyone in the bar that he was going to work me to death in the following two weeks. The first day Athel shore 110 and I shore 125. The next day he shore 120 and I shore 150. Try as he could, for the next 2 weeks, he could not keep up with me. By the end of the first week, he was not looking too good.

At first, everyone at Giltrap's took the piss out of him 'cause he'd bragged and skited that he'd shear more sheep than me. Halfway during the second week he looked terrible. His ego was crushed and he could hardly walk. He was overworking his body so much that people stopped teasing him and told him to slow down before 'old Yorky works ya into the ground'. He refused to listen and kept up his pace, hoping to catch up with me. At the end of two weeks, he had to visit the local doctor for some pills. A week later he had a heart attack and dropped dead. From that day on, some shearers claimed that Yorky was the only shearer in the Lake to work another shearer to death.

"Bullshit." I said.

| 7 |

Marking Lambs

On Monday morning at 10 to 6, I was sitting on Giltrap's steps waiting for Kevin Skippy to pick me up for a couple of days work, marking lambs.

"G'day, ya pommy fuckin' bastard." he yelled out the window as he pulled into the curb. "Chuck ya tucker box in the back and hop in mate."

"How are ya, ya Aussie fuckin' bastard?" I asked as we shook hands.

"Jeezus!" said Kevin, as he spun the wheels and left a small dust cloud behind us. "Ya really getting' our Aussie lingo down Yorky mate."

"Yeah, I've been gettin' a bit sick of people mimicking my Yorkshire accent and taking the piss out of me."

"Oh, don't worry about that sport. We've been extracting the urine out a' pommy's since they've been coming out here. Ask Stan Granthem, he speaks good Occa lingo now and we still take the piss! So, what have ya been up to Yorky? Ya got yourself a good root since ya been livin' in town?"

"No mate. No such luck in that department."

"What about some of those young Mission sheila's that hang out around Giltraps?"

"No mate, no luck there either."

"Ya still haven't had a root yet Yorky mate?"

"In one word Skippy, No!"

"I've got a pretty good-looking sheep in the backyard at our place. I could put a good word in there for ya, if ya like."

"Fuck you Skippy. I'm desperate but not that desperate."

"I don't blame ya." he said as he laughed out loud. "Anyway, it's too hard to pull their head around to kiss 'em!"

This little joke gave me a really good laugh as I said, "Oh mate, what a fuckin' great joke. I'm gonna remember that one."

"Good on ya Yorky mate. She's a pretty tough life out here in the Bush sport and a good joke never goes astray. They tell me ya gittin a few middys into ya self since you've been living at Traps."

"Yeah, there's not much else to do in the Lake if ya single."

"Ya not gonna end up like some of those old alcis' are ya?"

"'Course I'm fuckin' not. Just because I'm a pommy doesn't mean I'm stupid."

"You'll have to give me a few minutes to think about that one mate!"

"Fuck you Skippy." I said with a smile. "What we doing today anyway?"

"Marking lambs mate, before we fatten 'em up for the auction."

"I've never done it before, ya know."

"No worries mate, you'll be catching 'em, Digger's gonna mark 'em and I'm gonna' draft' 'em off and shift 'em back into the paddocks."

Pretty soon we were driving over the ramp at Skippy's property. I could already see a large mob of Ewes and lambs in an around the sheep yards. We parked the ute under a shady tree and walked towards the yards. Digger was filling up a back pack of drench. As soon as he saw me, he said, "Yorky, ya pommy bastard. How are ya cobber?"

"Good mate." I said as we shook hands. "Ya like living in town mate?"

"It's not bad mate. There's still not much to do though."

"I don't know about that Yorky. A little bird told me that ya rooting one of those pretty little half-cast ginns from out at the Mission."

"Bullshit Digger." I said. "Ya little bird's full a shit!"

"That's not what I heard Yorky. I don't wanna see ya sittin' on Shamen's corner with a couple a pic-a-ninis on ya knee next time I'm in town."

"Fuck you Digger, you're such a bull-shitter mate."

"Yeah, I know, but it's good fun Yorky.
You're always good for a laugh mate."

"G'day Yorky." said Dick as he walked over to where we were laughing and joking.

"Didn't ya bring that pretty little half-cast sheila I saw ya with on Saturday night?"

"Fuckin' hell Dick, you're just as bad as ya sons."

"Right, first time Yorky. Where d'ya think they git it from? Hey Kevin, bring that mob a' ewes and lambs in from the back boundary paddock, near Digger;s place. We'll git started on this mob. I'll draft 'em off while we're waitin' for ya."

"So, what d'ya want me to do Dick?" I asked. "Digger will show ya mate. He's the expert."

"Bullshit Dad, I'm the mug that ends up with the shitty end of the stick!"

"Come on Yorky mate. Let's git started." said Digger. "Sooner we start, the sooner we finish."

Digger and me walked over to a part of the sheep-yard fence that had a 2 foot long, 1-foot- wide plank that was screwed onto the top rail.

"Right mate, you catch the lambs after they're drafted off from the ewes and carry them over here. I'll go grab one and show ya how to hold 'em."

Digger grabbed hold of a lamb and carried it over to the fence.

"Alright, ya hold it like this mate, with his front and back leg together on each side. Ya sit his arse on the plank and push down a bit. Ya got it mate?"

"Looks easy enough to me Digger."

"It's easy at the beginning of the day Yorky, but by Sundown tonight ya hands will have cramp in 'em from the little bastards struggling. Grab hold of this one mate while I get on the other side of the fence."

As soon as Digger was ready, he said, "Now hang on to her mate!"

First up, he grabbed a pair of ear-marking pliers. He took hold of the lambs' ear and clipped a piece out of it which left their brand hole in it. The hole filled up with a small amount of blood.

"This is a ewe mate, so ear-mark and tail is all we do on this one."

Then he picked up a small, sharp-bladed knife which had 2 spring-like jaws for a handle. The spring jaws had serrated teeth on each side.

"Ya see this bit of bare skin under her tail, here right before the wool starts growing?"

"Yeah, what about it?"

"SWISH! Ya cut the tail off right there."

The tail came off quite easily as the knife was really sharp.

"If ya cut it too short mate, the blow-flys will get on its arse-hole and chances are they'll blow it."

"What happens then mate?"

"Maggots, mate. They'll start boring holes into and around its tucker-shoot. How d'ya like maggots boring into ya tucker chute Yorky?"

"Not fucking likely!" I said as Digger had a good laugh.

Digger dabbed a bit of tar on the lamb's tail and then said, "Let her go mate."

Once the lamb's feet were on the ground again, she ran around a bit, twitching her tail and ear, bleating for her mother. The next lamb I caught turned out to be a male.

"Jeezus mate, ya got a wether, or soon to be. Hold him steady mate." said Digger as he marked the opposite ear.

This time he cut the top of the lamb's ball-sack. Then he pushed back the ball-sack with his fingers and two small pink testicles popped out. What he did next, fuckin' shocked me. Digger put his head between the lambs back legs, grabbed one of the balls between his teeth and then pulled his head back. He now had a pink testicle in his mouth which had a small tube hanging off of it. Then he spit the testicle onto the dusty ground. Almost immediately one of the red Kelpies ran in, grabbed it and swallowed it in one gulp. Repeating the process, the lamb was now short his 2 small balls.

After he cut off the tail, he chucked it on the ground, dabbed the stump and empty ball-sack with tar and said, "Let it go Yorky mate. He's done."

The front of mi singlet had now acquired blood streaks, which came from cutting the tail off, all down the front. Each time a tail was cut, the hairline veins spurted out a thin stream of blood. I now had it on mi face as well as mi arms.

It wasn't long before the bush flies arrived, which by days end was torturous.

"Don't some cocky's put rubber rings on their balls and tail Digger?"

"Yeah mate, but that hurts 'em a hell of a lot more than this way."

"How d'ya know that mate?"

"Well mate, once ya let 'em up doing it this way, they run around and jump up and down a bit, right? Now when ya put a ring on their ball sack and tail, they run and jump a little bit and then they lay down on the ground for quite a while."

"Why's that Digger?"

"Why d'ya think mate."

"'Cause you've cut the blood supply off?"

"Right first time mate. It also takes a good few days for the nuts and tail to rot off."

"Fuck that for a game of tin soldiers Digger!

I'm fuckin' glad I'm not a sheep!" said Yorky.

Just then, old Dick came over and said to me, "I think when we've marked all these lambs Yorky, we'd better do you mate! It'll save ya havin' a swag of pic-a-ninis to look after. What d'ya reckon mate?"

"Fuck you Dick! My balls are staying right where they are, even though I haven't needed 'em yet!"

We all had a good laugh over that one till Digger said, "Alright Yorky mate, it's your turn. I'll go catch one for ya."

| 8 |

Redpath the Gun Shearer

I was introduced to a gun shearer, Ian Redpath. He was a tall bloke who always wore a pork-pie, punters hat when he wasn't shearing. He was mostly bald at the front of his head which made his appearance seem older than his years. A heavy drinking problem did nothing to correct it either.

Redpath was a quiet bloke until he had too much grog and then he could become very argumentative or he'd simply go to sleep on the bar stool with his head on the counter until the Publican decided he'd had enough rest then he'd wake him up. Upon waking, the first words out of Redpath's mouth were, "Give us another middy mate."

In town, Redpath was a hopeless drunk but when he got back in the sheds, after a couple of slow days he would be ringing the shed again. I became very fond of Redpath, despite his drinking habit. When he told me he was leaving the Lake to drive over to Western Australia, I asked him if I could go with him.

"No worries mate. Sling ya swag in the back of mi Ute. I'll be leaving tonight after Giltrap's closes."

It didn't take me very long to pack up mi case and as soon as Giltrap's did close, Redpath very casually sauntered out, carrying a dozen cans under his arm for the ride to Hilston where he was based.

We arrived in Hilston well after midnight. Instead of going to his room, which he rented at at a mate's house, he made his way to the back door of the Hilston Hotel. Once inside, we stayed there for at least 3 hours until the Publican refused to serve anymore beer. The following day, Redpath got up at 1 and headed towards the bar again. He kept this activity up for at least 3 days until I finally said to him, "I'm going back to the Lake mate. I didn't come with you to watch ya drink ya self to death. I'll be leaving as soon as I find a ride back."

This statement of mine must have given him a bit of a shock because he finished his beer, bought another dozen and said, "Alright, come on mate, let's hit the road!"

Pretty soon we were on our way with myself behind the wheel of his brand-new Ute. I knew he really liked me, otherwise he would have stayed at the bar drinking until he was broke. Also, he liked me to drive. No one lets a bloke drive his new Ute unless he enjoys his company.

We must have been on the road for around 6 hours. We'd changed seats and Redpath was now driving. Drunk or sober, he drove the Ute at around 80 miles an hour. Just as I was settling in for the long haul a big semi passed us on the dirt road. The next thing I heard was a loud 'BANG' as a stone shattered the windscreen to pieces. Immediately, Redpath applied the brakes and at the same time he pushed out a big enough hole in the windscreen, which enabled him to see where we were heading. As soon as the vehicle ground to a halt, we pushed out the whole windscreen. There was shattered glass all over the place.

"What a bastard!" said Redpath. "This calls for another beer!"

I cleaned up as much of the small pieces of glass as I could without a small dust pan and broom. When it looked all right to

Redpath he said, "Fuck it Yorky, that'll do sport. Open ya self a beer mate and we'll get moving again."

It's amazing how uncomfortable one can be in a Ute with no windscreen, especially traveling on a dirt road. Every car that drives past kicks up a huge amount of dry red dust.

When we finally reached a town called Wilcania, we were covered in a thick layer of dust from head to toe. Once we found the largest garage in town, the owner said he'd have to order a windscreen because it was a new Ute and he didn't carry spares for new vehicles. He also said that it would take at least 4 days before it arrived. Redpath ordered it and then drove straight to the Hotel to contemplate what to do, over a few cold middys.

That evening, as we made friends with a few of the local shearers, Redpath, who was known all over the Outback of NSW, managed to pick up some shearing and crutching for us. At least we'd make a few dollars while we waited in Wilcania. That evening, we drove out to a station called Mount Pleasant. It was anything but. There was only a few sheep to shear, so the rest of our time was spent crutching, daggy-arse sheep. Crutching consists of dragging out sheep, shearing the wool off of their rear-end in a fan-like shape.

Under normal conditions, one can make a lot of money out of crutching. Unfortunately, we were not crutching in ideal conditions. Once sheep have been let into a paddock that has plenty of green feed, they tend to get the scours. They shit all over the wool around their arse. Over a period of time, the blow-fly's, who see sheep shit as a five-star meal, land all over the sheep's arse. In the process, the blow-flys lay their eggs on the shit. After some time, the eggs hatch out as maggots. Maggots, being what they are, will look for food. Once they are firmly on the skin, they will start eating the sheep alive! They bore holes deep down into the sheep's rear end. If not caught in time, they will kill the sheep. Any shearer knows a fly-blown sheep. He can smell it. The antidote for this little trauma is to shear off all the wool where the maggots have been.

After he's done this, he yells out "TAR BOY!"

A roust-a-bout runs down the board to the shearer with a can of liquid, which he daubs all over where the blow-fly's have been, which stops them getting re-infected. The other operation that one encounters while crutching, is when the shit on the rear end of the sheep has dried hard as a rock. The only way to get this off is to chip away with the hand-piece until it's all gone. That was how we spent our time at Mt. Pleasant. After we finished our few days, he, luckily, found another 2 weeks shearing for us. It was decided that we'd forget about driving a few thousand miles across the Nullabar Plain and remain in Wilcania for as long as the work held out.

The following Friday evening Redpath and me drove back into town from a week's hard work in rough old wethers. We decided to try out one of the other bars, just for a change in scenery. We already knew quite a few shearers now which made the stay a bit more enjoyable. At around 9:30 I decided to go for a walk down the street for some fresh air. I was not interested in getting blind drunk with Redpath that night. Once I got outside a couple of Aborigine girls smiled a big smile at me and asked me my name and where I came from. Once I said, Lake Cargelligo, they asked me if knew all of their relations who lived out at the mission. After 10 minutes of talking, they suggested that after the bar closed down, if I bought some beer and wine, we could all go for a bit of a party out at the place they were living. I agreed to meet them later.

After I had a feed at the local Dago shop, I went back up to the bar to see how old Redpath was faring. By this time, he was firing on all 8 cylinders and was already quite argumentative when the Publican called 'Time' at 11. I told Redpath about the two Abo sheilas I'd met earlier. He seemed to like the idea 'cause he said, "At least it's somewhere to go where we can hang around and drink some more grog."

When we went around the back of the Hotel where Redpath had parked his Ute, the girls were waiting for us.

"G'day." they said as we approached. "Ya got some grog?"

"Of course I've got some fuckin' grog." said Redpath.

"Have ya ever known me not to have any?"

One of the girls said, with a smile, "How would we know? We've only just met ya mate."

"Then fuckin' go and ask anybody that knows me, they'll all tell ya the same thing. Ya might see old Redpath without food on many occasion but grog, you'll never see him without."

"Alright mate," said the older one. "Keep ya fuckin' hat on. We only asked."

"Where the hell are ya taking us anyway?" asked Redpath.

"Few miles out of town. Got a humpy out there. We can have a party without being disturbed." said one of 'em.

Once we were all squashed in the front seat of the Ute, he started it up and drove out of the car park and then up the main road. For some reason, he was driving very slow tonight which was totally out of character for him. He was driving so slow in fact, one of the girls said, "Can't this Ute go any fuckin' faster?"

"Course it fuckin' can. It's a brand-new Ute." he said. "What d'ya wanna go faster for?"

"Well mate, someone might see us with two white fellas."

"So fuckin' what?" said Redpath, who had now opened a new can.

"Don't worry me mate, but if the local cops see us with ya, you'll git into big trouble." said one of the girls.

"Fuck the cops. I've been in jail overnight more times than I can remember so once more won't make any difference to me." said Redpath.

At long last, we arrived at an old rusty, broken down tin shack at the end of a dirt track on the outskirts of town. When we went inside, I got quite a shock as I looked around. It was a one- room place with a dirt floor. The inside walls were just as rusty as the outside. The only furniture in the room was 2 single beds, one at each side of the room. On the actual bed part there were no mattresses, only a sagging chain- link spring affair which was supposed to hold at least a flock mattress. Instead, all that covered them were an old wool blanket. The only other furniture I could see was an old wooden chair which only had 3 legs. Redpath walked over to one of the beds and sat down on the edge of the frame with the booze at the side of him.

"Alright mate, give us a drink." said one of the girls to him.

"I don't know whether or not I should waste mi good beer on you Abo sheilas. Here, ya can open up this bottle of Plonk, if ya like."

"Is this where you live?" I asked. "Sure is mate. What else do we need?".

"Where d'ya cook?" I asked, 'cause there was no electricity or running water.

"Outside mate. We make a fire when we wanna cook up something."

"Where d'ya put ya clothes?" I asked.

"On mi body. Where else would I put 'em?"

"No, ya spare clothes." I said.

"What spare clothes is he talking about?" said the other girl.

"Fucked if I know." said the other one. "He must know something we don't."

"Are these thin cotton dresses the only clothes ya have?"

"Course they are. What do I need any more for? I can only wear one dress at a time."

"What d'ya do when ya have to wash 'em?"

"I wash it in the river and hang it over a bush till it dries, what else."

As we sat and talked, I asked them many questions about their lives. Most of the time, they thought I was pretty weird. Eventually Redpath started to talk politics to the girl who was now sitting next to him. He asked her for an opinion on the war in Vietnam.

"What you mean, 'Vietnam?' What war? Where about in New South Wales is Vietnam? I haven't never heard of it mate."

"What about all those young white kids that are dying over there so that you bastards can be 'free'?" said Redpath, who was now pretty drunk.

"What bullshit you fuckin' talkin' white fella?" she said.

"Maybe you had too much grog. Black fellas never have war. No white fellas ever die for black fellas but plenty black fellas die at the hand of white fellas. If ya so worried about this Bush town, Vietnam, why don't you go to war instead of gittin' on the grog?"

"Ya stupid, bloody Ginn." said Redpath, as he took another big swig out of his can. "Vietnam ain't in the Bush. It's another bloody country all together. Didn't ya learn anything at school?"

The girl who was now sat next to me said to him, "She never went to no white fellas school mate. She learn from tribal family everything about ancestors. Same as me mate. White fellas learning no good to black fellas. Only good thing white fellas have is plonk and Marlboros.

"Yeah, that's the bloody problem with you black bastards." said Redpath. "Ya never work or look after the land."

The girl who was sitting next to him took another swig out of the wine bottle and said, "What d'ya mean, black fellas not work or look after the land. Just look at you white fellas. You come to our land and in a few years it's almost dead! Ya put those chemical things on the land and then ya put up fences and tell us it's theirs and if we walk on it, we're trespassing. Then ya go and call the white fella sergeant on us."

"Ya can have ya land back for all I care." said Redpath, who was by now really drunk.

The Abo girl, who was now herself a bit drunk said to him, "We don't want it back now. You white fellas fucked it up so ya can have it. It's no good to us black fellas anymore."

As they were arguing back and forth, the girl who was sat with me said, "Come on mate, I wanna show ya something. Come outside."

When we got outside, she closed the door and then grabbed hold of my hand and took off at a fast pace into the Bush. After about 10 minutes of walking, we came to a big clearing in the Mall. The full moon was directly up above now and filled the clearing with a warm glow.

"Pretty place, eh?" she said as she looked around.

"Yeah," I said. "It's really peaceful out here."

"I wanna give you something very special." she said as she pulled off her dress. "You are a very special white fella. You are a very good man. Come on." she said as she laid down in the thick red dust. "Take off ya clothes and put it in here. I've got a gift for you."

We laid down in the Bush for at least 3 hours. When we were finished, I looked more like a black fella than a white one 'cause I was covered all over in layers of red earth.

"Let's go back now." she said. "The Sun will be comin' up soon. It's not good for you if white fellas see you with a black Gin."

When we got back to the tin humpy, Redpath was fast asleep in the front of his Ute. The other Abo girl was asleep on one of the rickety beds.

"You'd better wake him up and go now before some of my family show up."

It took me ages to wake up Redpath. When he eventually came too, he said, "Give us a middy mate!"

Come Sunday evening, Redpath and me drove back out into the Bush for another week's hard work shearing wethers.

The cook's name was Paddy Slaven. He was an old Irish immigrant with a bald head, fat round face and a chronic drinking problem. People who live in the Bush that have bad drinking problems are not called 'alcoholics' as long as they can get up and go to work every day but once the grog has really gotten hold of 'em and they can no longer work, then and only then are they branded as close to being an 'alcy'. Old Paddy was as close to being an 'alcy' as possible, without actually being labelled one. He drank from 5 in the morning until 11 at night, when he eventually ran out of grog. If he couldn't borrow a half-gallon of plonk, he would start on the Vanilla Essence. Many a contractor thought that Paddy would be baking a lot of cakes by the amount of Vanilla Essence he ordered for the stores but I can't remember ever eating one of Paddy's cakes.

When we finished that shed, we drove back into Wilcania for the weekend. On Saturday morning old Paddy was propped up at the bar drinking with one of his mates he'd met in town. By the time the afternoon arrived, he was broke down to the bones of his arse. When I walked into the bar, he made a bee-line for me. He gave me a sob story about having no money left for food. I was still pretty naive in those days. It only took old Paddy a few minutes to relieve me of a 10 dollar note, after promising to go to the Dago's shop and buy himself a good feed. When he walked away from me with the 10 bucks, I decided to keep an eye on him to make sure he didn't forget the purpose of the loan. As I watched him closely, he slid the 10-dollar bill over the counter for the Publican to change. When he got it back in two fives, he gave his drinkin' mate $5 and ordered another round of booze out of his 5. Once I saw that, I was really pissed! I walked over to where he was sittin' and said,

"Hey Paddy, ya told me ya wanted to buy ya self some food cause ya hadn't eaten for 24hours!"

"Yeah, Yeah Yorky. Ya know how it is mate."

"No I fucking don't Paddy. All I know is that you're a fuckin' liar! If I had known you were gonna blow it on booze, I'd have never given it to ya!"

"You'll git ya fucking money back mate. Why are ya so angry?"

"Cause you're a real fucking con-man Paddy and on top of that you're a chronic fuckin' alcoholic!"

"Don't ya fuckin dare speak to me like that ya pommy bastard!"

"Why Paddy, what ya gonna do about it. You'll never be sober enough to remember what I called ya."

"I'll knock ya arse over head in a minute." "You and who else Paddy, ya drunken alcy

mate? I could beat the shit out of both of ya with

one fuckin' arm. Anyway, I'll tell ya one thing for sure, ya fuckin' lush, If I ever saw ya starving in the gutter, I wouldn't piss on ya if ya were on fire. You're better off dead! As far as the 10 bucks go, ya can keep it Sport. From now on I'll warn everybody I know about ya, ya fuckin' conman!"

With that, I left him to his misery and went to the cafe, miself, for a good breakfast. I didn't very often get angry with people but that morning, if old Paddy had have pushed the issue too far I would have put him out of his fuckin' misery. I spent most of the afternoon playing pool and having a few beers with some of the shearers I'd met. As I was scanning the local paper, I read a small article about 3 blokes who'd killed themselves in a car crash on the outskirts of town. The article said that they were all blind drunk and had hit a Semi-trailer head on. The article's headline read, 'TWO MEN AND A SHEARER KILLED! That headline was the usual local attitude toward shearers or anyone who worked in the sheds.

Later on that evening, I saw the Aboriginal girl I'd met the week before. I took off into the Bush with her again before the long night was over. The following morning, as I was having a beer with Redpath, who was in a pretty bad state, the local Wilcania Sargeant appeared at the front door of the pub. I know, because I could see him in the large mirror behind the bar.

"Oye! You, ya bastard. Come out here.", he said.

Everyone in the bar turned around, except me. "Oye!" he said again. "If I have to come in
there and git ya, you'll be in deep shit mate!"

Slowly, I turned around on my stool and faced the front door.

"Yeh, you ya bastard. Come out here, I wanna a fuckin' word with you! G'day sport." he said in a nasty tone of voice.

"G'day, Sergeant what can I do for ya?" I said.

"Ya can't do a thing for me cobber but I've got a message for you!"

I had no idea whatsoever what the big, ugly Sergeant was talking about so I just kept quiet and waited.

"I understand from my source that ya fuckin' one of our local Gins." His nasty tone and bluntness took me by surprise, but only for a second. I said to him, "Your understanding from your source is wrong, Sargeant."

"I don't think so cobber, so listen to me and listen real good sport. If ya still in Wilcania by 1 o'clock this afternoon, I'll fucking lock ya up!"

"Why would ya do that? I haven't broken any of ya laws?"

"We've got a law in this town called 'Consorting'. If I was you sport, I'd get the fuck out-a this town and don't fuckin' come back!"

With that, he walked off down the street to where he'd parked the local blue Bull Wagon. When I walked back into the bar, Redpath, seedy as he was from his Saturday night binge said to me, "What did that big ugly bastard want?"

"He told me if I was still in town by 1 o'clock today, he was going to jail me for consorting."

"Fuckin struth!" said Redpath, who was now wide awake. "Let's grab a couple dozen bottles and git out of here before the ugly bastard comes back."

"Why, what does 'consorting' mean?"

"It means, ya not even allowed to talk to those black sheilas. If he finds out for sure that ya fucked one of 'em, he'll fuckin' lock both of us up and throw away the fuckin' key!" Redpath downed his middy in one large swallow. He paid the Publican for 2 dozen large bottles of Pilsner, then said to me, "Let's git our gear from the hotel and git out a here. I'm sick of this scungy, fuckin' town anyway!"

Once our swags were packed and put in the back of the Ute, we were once more on our way. We left Wilcania behind in a cloud of red dust. Redpath only drove a few miles before he said to me, "I'll pull over to the side of the road and you can drive, if ya like. This driving caper is interfering with a man's drinkin'."

When the Ute stopped, we exchanged seats. I pushed mi foot down on the accelerator and I said to Redpath, "Where to now mate?"

"I think we'll head off South, Yorky. We'll see if we can pick up a pen in those big, fat Corradale sheep. I'm a bit sick of shearing rough wethers. Besides, that Victorian Bitters is not too bad for a drop of grog. I haven't had any since last year. We'll head down to a place called Hamilton. I'll git the road map out and once we know where we're heading, I can relax and have a few beers while you drive."

On the way down to Hamilton, we stopped at a place called Horsham. Redpath ran into a contractor that he'd worked for a few years before. His name was Ron McClure. McClure was looking for one shearer. He had about six weeks' worth of work so Redpath took the pen. As we sat in the bar, I was starting to worry a bit because I had no work and no way of traveling without Redpath.

At the end of the evening Redpath said, "We're gonna stay at McClure's place tonight and tomorrow I'm gonna drive ya down to Hamilton. McClure says you're sure to pick up a pen shearing at this time of year. They're in full swing down there."

The following day, we took off early cause Redpath had to get back to Horsham. He dropped me off at the local shearer's pub. After I booked in, we had a couple of beers together. For all his problems, old Redpath had a big heart. Anyone else would have left me stuck in Horsham, but not old Redpath. After we said our goodbyes, he took off and I ordered another beer. I remember it was somewhere around 3 o'clock in the afternoon. I had another 3 hours to wait until the local shearers started to roll in. One thing about a shearer's pub is it doesn't take very long before one gets to know the local crowd. By

10 that evening, I'd met who a bloke who arranged a pen for me, starting in a few days. A couple of days later as we drove onto the cocky's place, I noticed the size of the sheep. A Merino sheep is usually pretty light unless they've been on real good tucker. These sheep I was now looking at were huge, woolly Coradale's, probably weighing around the 150-pound mark. The cocky was and old German called Shultz. Him and his son, who was about 22, ran the place. The shearers quarters were an old run- down house which had no electricity or fly screens on the windows. Because the grass around that area was long and green, mosquitos were a constant plague.

In the morning, I got into mi shearing gear and made mi way over to the main house for a bit of breakfast before I started. Shultz was also the cook. He told me his old lady had died a few years back and he was left to raise the boy on his own. At 7:30 I was loaded up and ready to start shearing. The shed was a small 2-stander and just after 7:30 another shearer turned up from town. He walked into the shed with his tucker box and a comb and cutter tin. As soon as he looked over the wall into his pen, he said to me, "Jeezus Christ mate, these fucking sheep look like baby elephants! I'll be flat strap shearing a fucking 100 a day in these bastards!" It took me all my my strength to drag the big, woolly Coradale ewes out of the holding pen, not to mention shearing them. I'd only been shearing for about a year but not consistently so my lack of experience did not enhance my ability to shear a good tally.

Normally, if I worked mi guts out all day, I could shear anywhere between 80 to 100 Merinos. After 2 hard hours of shearing old Shultzs' Coradales, I had only managed to poke out 15! The wool was really long and hard- cutting which meant I had to change the combs and cutters a lot. Because the sheep were so fat, they did not like being sat up or rolled on their backs. To show their disapproval, they kicked like hell. The bloke next to me cursed and swore as he sweated over the huge Coradales. By lunch time he had shorn 45. Once old Shultz was out of earshot, he said to me, "I'll be looking for another pen tonight when I git back to town. The bloke who told me about this place said they were not bad shearin'. Wait till I see that lyin' bastard again!"

"How long ya been shearin'?" I asked him. "15 years mate. How about you?"

"About a year, but not every week."

"You've only been shearin' a year mate? Jeezus sport, you're going real well in these mongrel bastards!"

"Not really. I'll be flat out getting 60 today." "But that's pretty good for a learner Yorky."

Look at me, I've only done 45. The last place I was at, I was shearing 150 a day."

"So ya think I'm going alright?"

"Listen mate, I'm one of the fastest shearers in Hamilton. Any bastard will tell ya that. As far as I'm concerned, if you can shear 60 for the day in these bastards, you're alright in my book sport."

At first, I was feeling really down cause I expected to shear at least 80 a day but this bloke on the stand next to me helped me feel a lot better about miself. He was a real supportive bloke. He stayed at the shed about a week before he pulled the pin on the old cocky. Over the next few days, he stopped several times to give me some good pointers on how to make the job easier for miself. On Friday night, I drove into Hamilton with him and booked into the Hotel. Over the weekend I met quite a few shearers in the barroom. Some of 'em were good blokes and some of 'em were real bastards. One bloke asked me how many a day I was shearing. When I told him 60, he started to laugh and take the piss out of me. As he was doing this, the shearer who had been working with me all week came into the bar. He was a well-known bloke around Hamilton. People greeted him as he waked in. When he saw me at the bar, he came over and said, "Drink up Yorky, I'll buy ya a beer mate."

"Good on ya." I said. "Good to see ya again," The shearer who had been taking the piss out of me knew the gun shearer who had just bought me a beer. He said to him, "Where ya been shearing at mate?"

"I've been shearin' with Yorky all week out at Shultz's place."

"How many ya doing a day there?" he asked him.

"90 was mi best day."

"Fuckin' hell sport, they must be real tough going for you to only shear 90 in 'em?"

"They fuckin' are." he said. "Old Yorky here was doin' as well as me for the length of time he's been shearing."

"Jeezus Christ." said the piss-taker. "I'm sorry for taking the piss out of ya mate. I didn't realize how tough a-goin' the sheep were."

The bloke I worked all week with said, "They been taking the piss out of ya Yorky, have they mate? Well don't let it worry ya sport cause these lazy bastards wouldn't shear 50 a day in those sheep. I'll put mi money on you any day of the fuckin' week mate. Drink up Yorky, I'll buy ya another beer."

From that point on, no one else took the piss out of me. In fact, I had a pretty good time in Hamilton the 6 weekends I spent there. After the bar closed down at 10:30, I made mi way out to the lounge. The lounge was open at least another 3 hours for residents and their guests. I met a shearer called Brian Cullen. Brian was a pretty big, strong bloke who came from Cunnamulla. We hit it off right from the beginning. That made mi stay there a lot more comfortable. Once that shed was finished, I left a message for Redpath at McClure's place. He returned my message sayin', 'Hitchhike up to Horsham. I've got a pen for ya, shearing with me.' The message made me feel really good. I packed up mi case, paid mi bill at the bar and made mi way up to the Hotel in Horsham where I found Redpath, full as a boot, proppin' the bar up. Redpath was very supportive of my shearing efforts.

The following day we drove out to the Bush to start another shed. One weekend, whilst hanging out in the bar, I met a bloke, Clay O'Malley. He was a handsome-looking bloke with wide shoulders and a reputation to match. He was very popular with the sheilas and the contractors for his respective talents. Redpath and me were sat quietly at the bar drinking a cold beer when he made his grand entrance. Modesty was not one of O'Malley's better qualities. Before long, he was bragging about the amount of sheep he could shear, the amount of sheilas he'd had and the amount of grog he could hold. During his bragging session, the subject somehow got on to snakes. As expected, O'Malley was also an authority on poisonous snakes. To prove it, he said he'd head out into the bush and catch one. The Publican told him not to be so stupid because he had too much grog in him. True to form, O'Malley would not have a bar of it. He downed his beer in one mouthful, picked up his change, then made his exit from the bar.

Whilst he was gone, no one gave it another thought because most people were used to his ways. It wasn't until he made his grand entrance again, carrying a small sugar bag that anyone took him seriously.

"Give us another middy." he said to the publican as he sat down on the bar stool and put the sugar bag on top of the bar.

"What's in the bag Clay?" said Redpath, who was not at all keen on snakes.

"It's a copper-head mate?"

"Oh Bullshit!" said Redpath, who was now sliding his stool a couple more feet to the right of the bag.

"I tell ya, it's a copper-head mate. As soon as I've finished this beer, I'll get it out and show you. O'Malley didn't wait to finish his beer, instead he slid his bar stool back from the counter and started to undo the string which held the top of the sugar bag securely tied. Once the string had been loosened, he held it closed with his left hand.

"Now I'll show you bastards what's in the bag!" he said as he felt around the outside of it. "Ah, here we go!" he said as he held onto something from the outside. "I've got hold of his head now. I'm gonna put mi hand inside the bag and pull him out!"

Everyone, including myself, stepped back at least another 3 feet as he let go of the bag opening. O'Malley pushed his hand, very carefully, into the bag as we all looked on. Just then he pulled his hand back out at great speed and said, "Shit! Bastard! He fuckin' got me!"

"What d'ya mean, 'he got me'?" said Redpath.

"I thought I had hold of his head securely but he wriggled free and bit me thumb!" he said as he closed the bag tightly.

"Hurry up!" he said in a panicked voice. "You've gotta get me to a hospital!"

Redpath, drunk as he was, sprang into action! "Alright, hurry up mate. My Ute's outside. I'll take ya! The publican told us where the closest hospital was. Before we went any further, O'Malley cut his thumb and tied a piece of string around it as fast as he could. In no time at all, we were doing 90 miles an hour up the wide bitumen highway towards the hospital. On the way, O'Malley kept saying to me, "Undo the tourniquet and move it up a bit and then pull it as tight as ya can."

Once this was done, he said, "Well, it looks like I'm really fucked now. I'll never make it cause once the tourniquet's up to the top of mi arm, there's nowhere else to tie it!"

Redpath drove like a first-class racing car driver as he steered the Ute around the wide corners with the needle bouncing on 105, most of the time. Before long, I had made the last tie, just below the shoulder muscle in O'Malley's left arm.

"That's it. We can't move it again. I'm out of time mate! I always wondered how I was gonna die. Now I don't have to wonder anymore."

"You'll be alright mate." I said. "Don't worry, there's not too far to go now!"

"How far to go, Redpath?" asked O'Malley. "Twenty miles mate but at this speed it won't take long."

"I'm fucked! Now I'm really fucked! Tell mi old lady what happened will ya and do what ya can for mi kids."

O'Malley was now starting to get groggy. His eyes started to close and his breathing became shallow and slower.

"Don't let me go to sleep." he said in a whisper. "Keep me awake."

The only thing I could think to do was to slap his face and shake him.

"Tell me how many sheep ya shore last week mate?" I said.

"I was the fastest in the shed." he said softly. "Just as fuckin' well for you that I wasn't

shearing next to you, ya gutless bastard. I'd have run rings around ya!" I said. This statement brought him back a bit, so I pursued it further. "The only problem with you fucking Aussies is ya full of shit and ya got no balls. A fuckin' good pommy could blow ya arse off, in a shed!" I said, as his head lolled from side to side. "Wake up, ya gutless bastard!" I screamed at him as I slapped his face from side to side.

"That fuckin' hurts." he said in a soft whisper.

"That's because you've got no fuckin' guts O'Malley. You're all fuckin' talk and no action!" I yelled in his face.

"I could work you into the ground, ya fuckin' pommy bastard." he said as his head lolled forwards.

"You haven't got the fuckin' balls O'Malley!" I screamed at him. I pulled his head up and I slapped his face around a bit more.

"Hospital's coming up on the left." said Redpath. "Smack him around a bit more mate. Don't let him drift off!"

As we pulled up outside the Emergency entrance, a couple of doctors were waiting with a wheel chair. The publican had called ahead and everyone was fully prepared for him. It only took seconds before he was out of the Ute and into the wheelchair heading for the front door. Redpath and me parked the Ute and then went into the Emergency waiting room to wait for some information.

After about an hour, a doctor came out and said, "He's gonna be alright now. We gave him a shot of anti-venom and he's sleeping peacefully. It's a good job you kept him conscious, cause if not, he'd be dead by now."

"How long will he be kept in?" asked Redpath.

"At least 5 hours or so. We want to make sure he's alright before we let him go."

We decided there was no more we could do. We filled up the Ute with petrol and drove back to the hotel, only this time the speedo needle never got above 60.

"You're not a bad driver." I jokingly said to Redpath.

"You're not a bad psychologist. Ya really got his attention when ya called him a gutless bastard and told him ya were gonna run rings around him if ever you were in the same shed together."

"Yeah mate, but I wouldn't dare tell him that, had he been alright."

"Fuckin' hell no. He's knocked some real big men arse over head for just looking sideways at him."

"Oh shit. I hope he doesn't remember!"

Late that afternoon, O'Malley made another grand entrance into the barroom. This time his thumb was bandaged and his ego was a bit bruised.

"Are ya alright mate?" I asked him.

"Course I'm fucking alright. I'm an Aussie. If it had been a pommy bastard that'd gotten bit, he'd have been dead by now."

Redpath piped up, in a drunken slur, and said, "If it wasn't for this pommy, you'd have been one big, dead, fuckin' Aussie. I think you owe us, at least, a round of beer so quit your skiting and put ya fuckin' money where ya mouth is!"

"We'll have 2 more middys publican." said O'Malley.

Not long after that Redpath and me did a couple of sheds in South Australia at a place called Narrow Court. We both lost a good few bucks on a horse called Tobin Bronze. According to Redpath, he could not lose! After that, we drove to a place called White Cliffs where they mine for Opal. There was not much work around by now. Redpath told me to go to Broken Hill 'cause he was gonna get on the grog for at least a week. He said he'd had it with shearing for a while. Redpath was a fair-dinkum gun shearer. I learned a few good blows from him as far as shearing Merino's goes, in the 4 or

5 sheds we shore together. I said goodbye to Redpath the following day and got a ride with the mail truck to Broken Hill. I never saw Redpath again after that. I firmly believe that if he's still alive, he can be found propping up the bar at the Hilston Hotel in New South Wales!

| 9 |

Broken Hill with Soreback & Cream

Broken Hill is a city in the desert. It is a pretty big place according to the mailman and sported at least a hotel on every street corner. Mining, gambling, shearing, Two-Up and drinking were the main activities of this city in 1968. I was 19 years old then and every day I shore, I was getting faster and cleaner. The mailman told me of a bar where all the shearers drank at, but, he said, The Argent Hotel was the best place to stay, so I took him at his word. He dropped me off outside the Argent and I thanked him for the ride and offered to buy him a beer next time I saw him.

The owner of the Argent was a greek. Nick the Greek, they called him. He was a very friendly bloke. As soon as I spoke a few words of Greek to him, his face lit up and our friendship was established.

One of the characters I met in the Argent was a black fella who went by the name of Soreback. Soreback was a short man and very heavy. He must have weighed 250 pounds, if he weighted a pound. He was totally bald on top and his eyes bulged out slightly, probably because of the amount of grog he used to consume. Old Soreback told me his name was Ralph Horton and that his mother was a Maori from New Zealand. I had no reason to not believe him until a bloke told me he was a half- caste Abo. His real name was Ralph Hampton from Uabalong, a town outside of Lake Cargelligo. The bloke told me Soreback had a brother called Buddha Hampton, who I had met on many occasions in Giltrap's Hotel.

Old Buddha was always in trouble with the cops when he got on the grog. So much so, it was rumoured around the Lake, that his death was caused by a severe beating from 3 big cops. The version the police put out was that Buddha Hampton had a heart attack in jail overnight. I never said anything to Ralph as I really liked him a lot. It was obvious to me that, for whatever reason, he didn't want anyone to know of his past. As far as I was concerned, I met him as 'Soreback' and I called him Soreback over the years that I knew him.

Soreback normally lived in New Zealand's South Island, at a place called Cheviot. He had come over to Australia because a friend of his from Cheviot, whose name was Cream, wanted the experience of shearing Aussie Merino sheep. Cream was just as big a drinker as Soreback. They both spent their time and money drinking for hours on end at the Argent bar. Cream had just finished his first Merino shed. As soon as he had a few beers under his belt, he could not stop talking about the shock he'd received when he tried to shear Merinos.

Over the next couple of days, fate arranged it that, I was to work in a shed with Soreback and Cream as a cook until the contractor could find one. Once he found a cook, he said he'd give me a pen, shearing. Soreback, Cream and myself drove out to the shed that was miles and miles out in the Bush. The place was called Milperinca. On the map of NSW, it's a tiny little dot, north of Broken Hill. Milperinca was the name of the sheep station. There was nothing around us for hundreds of miles but Bush. The first morning, I was up bright and early so I could light the wood stove. I made up a breakfast of bacon, eggs, lamb chops and toast. The bloke who was running the shed for the contractor told me that I'd done a good job at making breakfast but a few of the shearers were big, militant trouble-makers.

By lunch time they were complaining about the quality of my cooking. The bloke running the shed, Mick Rice, said to me, "Tell ya what we'll do Yorky. It's pretty easy to see that those complaining bastards, for whatever reason, don't like ya. We won't tell 'em but I'll do the cookin' for this evening's meal and we'll just let 'em think that you've done it. That way, we'll get through the shed with no complaints."

That afternoon, Mick cooked up a roast with potatoes, cabbage, onions and gravy. When dinner-time came, I served up the meal, just as if I'd cooked it. As soon as the meal was over, the same 4 blokes pulled Mick over to the side and told him the meal was shit and they weren't paying good money to eat rotten cooking. When Mick told me what had happened, I asked him why he didn't tell 'em that he'd done the cooking. "Won't do no good Yorky. They've got a set on ya and they won't be happy until you're out of the kitchen."

The following day, instead of cooking breakfast, I was given the job of roust-a-bout, for the rest of the week. I was much happier in the shed but I would have preferred to be shearing instead of picking up wool. Old Soreback was having a hard time of it. Every time he got to the last side of the sheep, he would straighten up his back for about 20 seconds, then he'd continue to finish the sheep. Between sheep, he would be in the catching pen, spewing up a colorless liquid and coughing like hell. I've seen a lot of shearers in pain in my days but none as bad as Soreback was.

"Hey Yorky."

"What d'ya want Soreback?"

"Shear one for me will ya while I pick up a bit of wool for ya?"

"I'd love to Soreback!" I said as I pulled out a sheep.

The biggest trouble-maker at the shed was a tall, black-haired bloke called Ron Cole. He was shearing on the stand next to Sorebacks. As soon as he saw me pull out a sheep, he gave me a dirty look. I shore 5 sheep for Soreback and by the time I'd warmed up, I was now keeping up with Cole, blow for blow. He didn't like that one bit. At lunch time he complained to Mick Rice that Soreback wasn't doing my job well enough. Rice had no other option but to tell me not to shear any more sheep for Soreback. The end of Milperinca shed found Soreback, Cream and myself, back at the Argent Hotel. There was a space at the bar next to two of the shearers, who had been shearing at the same shed with us. One of the bloke's name was Bill. He was one of the roughest-looking characters that I'd ever seen. He was around 50 years of age. He had a nose that had been broken at least a couple of times and a long scar on his cheek.

"G'day Bill." I said. "How're ya doin' mate?" "Not bad Yorky, Now I've got a few middys under mi belt."

As the Publican was pulling 3 middys for us, Ron Cole, who had been drinking at the end of the bar, casually walked over to where I was standing. From the look on his face, I knew he was going to start causing problems for me. The first words out of his mouth were, "I don't drink at the same bar as pommy, fuckin' bastards!"

Before I could say a word, Bill put his middy down, took out his top and bottom false teeth and said to his mate, "Here, hold these for me and don't fuckin' drop em!" He then turned to Cole and said, "Why don't ya put ya fuckin' beer down you Yankee fuckin' bastard, cause I'm gonna knock you arse over fuckin' head! I'm just about sick of you riding this young fella for the whole shed!"

"Ya no need to be like that!" said Cole, as his face turned white and fear showed in his eyes.

"I won't tell ya again, ya Yankee, fuckin' bastard! Git out of this fuckin' hotel now and do your drinking somewhere else! Ya got half-a- fuckin' minute mate, to make ya mind up, then you'll be on the deck!"

Cole downed what was left of his middy and put his glass down on the bar. He turned around and walked over to where he'd left his drinking mate who, in turn, downed his beer in a hurry. Both of them walked out of the Argent Hotel together. Bill turned to his mate and said, "Ya got me teeth there, Sport?"

His mate handed him both sets.

"Good on ya." said Bill, as he stuck 'em both in his mouth.

"I didn't wanna keep 'em in, in case that Yankee bastard got in a lucky blow."

"Thanks a lot Bill." I said. "That was real good of ya mate."

"No worries Yorky, I've been wanting to do that for the whole fuckin' shed. It's a pity the Yankee Bastard wouldn't step up. I was looking forward to stoushin' that loud-mouthed bastard."

"Can I buy you and ya mate a beer?"

"There's no need Yorky, but if ya want to, I won't refuse! And while we're at it mate, ya see that bloke, the other side of the bar, the one with the cast on his arm? He's a fuckin' con man mate! When he sees ya' on ya' own, he'll come over and put the bite on ya. Don't give the bastard a brass razoo."

"How come mate?"

"Cause there's nothin' wrong with his arm. He's a good-for-nothin' no-hoper. He puts that cast on his arm every shearing season and makes the rounds of the hotels spinnin' a bullshit yarn."

"Thanks for tellin' me, I'll keep mi wits about me."

| 10 |

Bombs Away

I'm now 35 years old now. Six o'clock, Monday morning, found me sitting on the steps of the Hotel waiting to be picked up by the contractor. I was looking at an hour's drive as we were doing a suburban shed for a couple of weeks.

While I was waiting, I did a quick check on mi gear. Tool box with combs, cutters etc. Esky box with enough tucker to get me through the day, water bag and last but not least, a sweat towel which was guaranteed to be used. Everything in my life revolved around the hotel. I lived there, found my work there and got dropped off there at the end of the day. The first car of the morning pulled up and out got Johnny Prisk, the 'penner upper' along with two red kelpies. His missus handed him his tucker box, then gave me a wave as she pulled away from the curb.

"G'day Yorky Mate. How are ya?"

"Not bad Prisky. How are you mate?"

"Pretty good Yorky. I had an early night last night."

"Does that mean ya got ya leg over mate?" I asked him.

"Not bloody likely. I've been married for 15 years. The last time I got mi leg over, I woke up with the guilts! I thought I'd committed incest."

This little joke gave us both a good laugh.

"Grab ya gear Yorky. Here comes the contractor."

"Yorky, Prisky, how are ya?" said the contractor as he got out of his newly leased sedan.

"Stick the dogs in the boot Prisky. We've got three more blokes to pick up."

"What! I'm not putting 'em in the boot! It's an hour's drive out to this Cocky's place."

"Well ya not puttin' 'em in mi new car! I've only had it a couple of days."

"Then fuck it! I'm not startin, I'll go back home to my place. I've got enough work on my property to keep me goin' for a week at least." said Prisky.

After arguing back and forth for five minutes, it was decided the dogs would travel in the car, on the floor, in the back. Once all the blokes were on board, we headed out of town and onto the dirt road.

"Yorky! Ya pommy bastard." said Dudley, who was one of mi good mates. "Did ya git on the piss last night?"

"I had a few but I wasn't legless."

"What about you mate? Were ya drinkin' at the Golf Club?" I asked.

"Yeah, but I left early. I was pissed-off. I done a hundred bucks on the game. I gotta' stop that gamblin' caper. I always seem to lose!"

"Yeah, it's a mugs game Dudley."

"I heard, over the weekend that you shore 237 lambs at Sanson's property last week."

"That's right mate."

"They must have been good shearin' eh?" "Course they were Dudley. We can't all be gun shearers like you mate!"

"Git fucked Yorky!"

"By the way Yorky, someone told me you were tryin' to root my sister at that party on Saturday night."

"That's bullshit Dudley, I only had a couple of dances with her."

"Well if ya do get onto her Yorky, make sure ya use a condom. I don't want a Pome bastard for a brother-in-law! It's enough that I've got to shear with one."

"Fuck you Dudley, I'm the best shearin' mate you've had."

"Sit down, ya bastard!" said Paul, one of the other shearers.

"What are these fuckin' dogs traveling in the car for? Why aren't they in the boot?"

"Fuck you!" said Prisky. "My dogs aren't ridin' in the boot for an hour on a dirt road!"

"All right, settle down you blokes." said Jack, the contractor. "You're at each other's throat already and we're not even halfway there yet!"

A few more miles down the road, another shearer called Herb said to me, "Hey Yorky, did you just drop ya guts?"

"NO! I fuckin' didn't. I thought it was you!" I said.

"It's those fuckin' dogs." said Dudley. "And the bastards are right under my feet."

A minute later, one of the dogs dropped one of the most vile farts I've ever smelled.

"Fuck me dead!" said Herb. "Stop the fuckin' car and let me out or I'm gonna' chunder on the floor!"

"SHIT!" said Jack the contractor. "Mi new car's gonna' smell like a dog pen!"

The car came to an abrupt halt, all four doors opened and a shearing team exited the car a lot faster than they got in. All the blokes stood on the side of the road in a cloud of dust, spitting and coughing. Big Paul actually lost a couple of middies from the night before. All the while this little drama was playing out, Prisky's dogs had climbed up on the back seat to see what all the commotion was about.

"What the fuck have you been feedin' these mongrel-bred bastard dogs?" said Jack."

"They're pure-bred Kelpies mate, not mongrels!" said Prisky. "And if you must know they've been livin' on roo meat for the past week."

"No fuckin' wonder!" said Big Paul. "You owe me a couple of middies when we get back to town Prisky and furthermore there's no way I'm traveling in this car while those fuckin' dogs are in the back!"

"That'll do!" said Jack. "Like it or not Prisky, the fuckin' dogs are goin' in the boot and that's that! Tomorrow, you can drive ya own car out and I'll pay for the petrol. It's either that or walk home mate!"

Reluctantly, the dogs were relegated to the boot and Prisky had now, well and truly, got the shits. It took another five minutes or so, with the doors and windows open, before it was humanly safe to get back in the car and be on our way.

At last, we arrived at the shed. After we'd signed on and drawn lots, I ended up on number four stand which was close to the door but I had a good drag to the stand. Once the bell went, we were off! After I'd shorn 9 or 10 wethers, I reckon if I kept up this pace all day I would probably end up with around 130 which wouldn't be too bad a tally for wrinkly weathers covered in wool.

Everything was goin' well until the second half of the first run when the cocky walked into the shed. He came straight over to my stand and fuckin' bombed me, "Ya need to clean 'em up around the head better mate." he said and then took off again.

Once I'd finished the wether I was on I shoved it down the shute and looked out the window at the sheep in mi counting-out pen. They looked pretty good to me and I'm my own worst critic. At the end of the run, I went up to the contractor and had a word with him. "Hey Jack, when you count my pen out, check 'em out for me will ya"?

"No worries Yorky mate. Why? Is there a problem?"

"Yeah, that fuckin' bastard cocky bombed me for not cleanin' 'em up around the head! Can you fuckin' believe it?" I told him.

"No worries mate. I'll check 'em out out for ya."

During smoke the contractor said to me, "I checked out ya sheep Yorky. They're good enough for me mate."

At the beginning of the next run, I'd only shorn one sheep and the fuckin' cocky was at my stand again, telling me there were too many ridges around the neck.

"They're fuckin' wrinkles!" I said. "My sheep are just as well-shorn as anyone elses!"

Soon as he'd left the shed, I walked over to Dudley's stand and asked him if he'd swap stands for about 10 sheep. After I explained what was happening Dudley said, "No worries Yorky!"

We had just swapped stands back when the cocky came over to stand and bombed me again. I was coming down the last side so I pulled out of gear, disconnected the hand-piece and said to the cocky, "So my sheep are not shorn well enough for you, is that right?"

"That's right! they're not clean enough."

"No worries sport. Take a look at mi mate Dudleys' sheep. Tell me if his sheep are cleaner than mine?"

As we walked over to Dudley's stand, he had just let his first one go.

"Right mate, what about those sheep? Are they good enough for ya?" I asked him.

The cocky surveyed Dudley's pen of shorn weathers for a half minute or so and said, "Yep! they're good enough for me. That how I wanna' see your sheep shorn!"

"You mongrel-bred fuckin' cunt! Those are my sheep! I shore those! Dudley and miself swapped stands. Only one of those well-shorn bastards are his! The other fuckin' 9 are mine!"

"Bullshit!" said the cocky. "You can't shear that many that clean!"

Now I was really fuckin' angry and Dudley said, "He's right mate. Yorky shore those sheep. We swapped stands for 10 sheep."

He turned to me and said, "I don't care who shore 'em! I want you off my property!"

By this time the conversation had gotten well and truly out of hand. Just then the contractor appeared and said, "What the fuck is goin' on?"

"This mongrel fuckin' cunt has bombed me three times so me and Dudley changed stands for 10 sheep and this bastard is still sayin' the sheep in my pen are not clean enough when in fact, these are my sheep here!"

"What's the problem Phil?" Jack asked the cocky.

"I don't like his shearing. They're not clean enough!"

Jack looked out the window into the pen and said, "Well, there's Yorky's sheep and they look really well-shorn for me mate."

"I don't care!" said the cocky. "I want him off my property!"

That was it! I'd had enough of this bastards bullshit so I grabbed him by the front of his shirt and slammed him against the shed wall. I'd still got mi handpiece in mi hand so I put it about an inch from his windpipe and said, "Go on you mongrel cunt, open ya mouth again and I'll ram this fuckin' handpiece straight through ya adam's apple, ya fuckin' poofta!"

"Whoa!" said the contractor. "Steady on there Yorky mate, don't do it! He's not worth it!"

"Shove ya mongrel bred weathers up ya fuckin' dung funnel ya gutless cunt and don't let me see ya in the shearers pub or I'll knock ya arse over head, ya gutless bastard!" I said.

Once mi gear was packed up, the contractor came over and said, "Jeezuz Yorky, I thought for sure you were really gonna' kill him."

"Not really mate, but I bet ya he's got to change his strides! No bastard disrespects me like that, especially when he said Dudley's sheep were well shorn and I actually shore 'em. So, how do I get back to town now Jack?"

"Take my car Yorky. We'll all pile into one car and don't hit any roos with it. It cost me a fortune to lease."

"Ya got a pen for me tomorrow mate?" I asked him.

"Yeah, no worries there mate. I'll swap one of mi other blokes around."

"What's wrong with the bastard Jack? Why'd he pick on me?"

"He just took an instant dislike to ya. It's got nothing to do with ya shearing mate. That just an excuse."

That night in the bar it was beers all round and everyone had a good laugh.

"Jeesuz Yorky mate," said Dudley as he handed me a middy. "I thought for sure that fuckin' cocky was a gonna'."

"Me too mate." I said and downed mi beer in a couple of gulps. "Come on Dudley, ya fuckin' Aussie bastard. Drink up or a pome shearer will be drinkin' ya under the bar."

"No fuckin' way will a pome drink me under the bar!", said Dudley. "And don't forget what I told you this mornin'...Stay away from my sister!"

| 11 |

Off to New Zealand

Old Soreback was one of those shearers that before the night was out, he was broke. He never had a razoo to his name. Needless to say, as soon as we left, I loaned Soreback a hundred bucks which he promised to pay back at the end of his next shed. Before Saturday night was over, Soreback had blown the 100 bucks I'd loaned him on the afternoons racing, so he bit me for another 50. The weekend arrived again and mi shed was finished. From all accounts, work around Broken Hill would now be in short supply.

I was having a beer with Soreback and Cream when Soreback announced, "I've had enough of this fuckin' place! I'm thinking I'll go home to New Zealand."

"Yeah, me too." said Cream. "These bastard sheep are too good for me!"

"When ya planning on leaving, Soreback?" I asked.

"Soon as I get the shearing contractor in New Zealand to send me some money for a ticket." By now Soreback was into me for $300. I casually asked him about the money he owed me.

"Don't worry about it Yorky. Soon as I get working in Cheviot again, I'll send ya the money to wherever ya like. Ya know, you could come over to New Zealand with mi, if you want to."

I'd never thought about leaving Australia but as soon as old Soreback mentioned it, I considered the possibilities and said, "Yeah, why not mate! I can only think of going back to Lake Cargelligo and there's not lot of shearing around there this time of year."

The decision was made. Over the next few days, we booked a flight from Broken Hill to Sydney which arrived at 4 in the afternoon. The flight to New Zealand left the following day at 2 pm. Flying across NSW in a plane was my first air flight. It was an incredible experience to look down and see all the dry, bush country that I'd wandered around in for the past 4 years. I felt more than a little sad as the plane crossed the vast outback. City living was not for me. When the small plane touched down at Kingston-Smith airport in Sydney, life took on a completely different turn.

"Where we gonna stay tonight Soreback?" I asked.

"There's a cheap hotel at Kings Cross. I stayed there on the way over. I can't remember the name but I do remember the huge neon Coca Cola sign at the top of Williams street."

The hotel was a pretty clean place and not too expensive for one night in the heart of Kings Cross. Once we'd dropped our gear off at the room, we all went back downstairs to look over the Cross. We found a comfortable bar with a big window. We could relax and watch the procession of prostitutes walking up and down the streets. Later on that evening we went for a good meal. Soreback suggested we take a walk around the brothels to see what action was going on.

In 1968, there used to be rows and row of terraced houses off of Williams Street. Every single one of those houses was a whore house. As we walked around the streets, women of all ages, sizes and shapes sat in the front windows of the houses. Most of them were clad only in thin, see-through negligees. Some of them were completely topless. As we walked around, with the hundreds of other people, some of the whores would smile and crook a finger in our direction. A lot of the women I was seeing were really hard-faced and wore tons of makeup, trying to hide the life of pain and suffering they were leading. Every now and then I'd see a decent looking woman. I guessed she mustn't have been in the business very long. Old Soreback was 59 at the time. As soon as he saw a woman that he fancied he said, "Jeezus, look at the tits on that sheila. I think I'll go in for a closer inspection."

"You're not serious are you Ralph?" I asked.

"Course I'm fuckin' serious. I've got plenty money in mi pocket and we're only in town or one evening so why not? I'll see ya both back at the hotel later."

With that, Soreback headed for the front door. When the woman with the huge knockers saw Ralph coming, she climbed out of the window, opening her legs as she went. A few seconds later she appeared at the door and Soreback disappeared inside.

"How the fuck can he do that?" I said to Cream.

"I don't know mate. When we first came over from New Zealand, I went into a place miself. It was the worst experience of mi life but old Soreback loves 'em. He must have spent at least a third of his money in these places."

Once Cream and me had finished looking around, we headed back up the Cross to the bar where we'd arranged to meet Soreback. Cream, whose real name was John Burnett, was a very quiet bloke until he'd had a few too many beers. Once he was full, his personality changed quite radically. Not that he got violent or anything like that. The more beer he consumed the more stupid he became. His voice used to change and all these weird characters would start to come out of him. Over the years I knew him, he only once flew off the handle. Old Soreback had him pretty well under control.

Around midnight, Soreback came back to the hotel bar where we were waiting for him. Cream and I kidded him about his sore back. When he was shearing, he always had to straighten his back before he could finish the sheep. I said to him, "Hey Ralph, did ya have to get off and straighten ya back before ya finished her off?"

"Don't be silly mate. Mi back's never felt better in mi life. In fact, I think I'll have a few more beers and go back for another go. Maybe I'll try a different one this time."

Back at the hotel, we had a large room with 3 single beds in it. The following morning, I was up real early. When I looked around, old Soreback's bed was empty. He must have been up all night. At around 6:30 he arrived back at the room. He was pretty drunk. The back of his shirt was out and his dark, bulging eyes were blood-shot red.

"D'ya have a good night Soreback?" I asked.

"Shit yeah, course I did Yorky. Ya never know mate, I may never come this way again so I made the best of a night in Kings Cross."

Old Soreback had now gone through most of the money the contractor in New Zealand had sent him. He bit Cream for a hundred bucks and we all took off up the Cross to the Bourbon and Beef Steak for a hearty breakfast of T-bone steak and eggs. By the time the afternoon came I was ready to go to the airport. I had a lot of fun walking around the Cross but it was not a place that I would've liked to live. I was quite happy and relaxed as we made our selves comfortable on the Air New Zealand plane. The Pilot's voice came over the intercom and gave us a few bits of information like travel time and weather.

Once he was finished, the seat belt sign flashed on and the Jet taxied down the runway. A few minutes later the nose of the plane was pointing skywards and we're on our way to New Zealand...

| 12 |

Sad News

After getting off a flight in Christchurch, I made mi way to the Newman's bus depot to catch a bus to Cheviot in North Canterbury. When I walked into the Cheviot Hotel, most of mi old shearing mates, from seasons gone by, were in the bar drinking and playing darts which was their habitual activities.

The first bloke who saw me was Cream, who I had first met in Broken Hill with mi old mate Soreback.

"Yorky, ya old bastard! How are ya mate? When did ya get back and where ya been since last season?"

"I just finished a season in Aussie, mate. I was shearing in England and Scotland before that. Where's Soreback mate?"

"Oh fuck Yorky mate, Ya haven't heard eh?"

"Heard what?"

"Ya old mate Soreback had a heart attack about nine months ago. He was shearing at a shed in Amberly one day and they found him dead in bed the following morning."

"Fuck me dead Cream, that's a bit of a shocker!"

"Too fucking right Yorky, it was a shock for me too. Ya know he lived at my place for 6 years. For the first month after he died, I got blind drunk every night. I couldn't handle the emotional upset. Every night when I went home, the house was empty and I only had miself to drink with."

"Did the Doctor know why he had a heart attack?"

"He said it was too much booze and he was grossly over-weight for his height."

The fact that old Soreback was dead caused a rush of memories to flood into mi mind. I remembered all the times we'd shorn together, the horse races we went to, all the parties and Barbecues we shared. In those wild days, as a young man, the thought of death never occurred to me much.

As far as I was concerned, everyone I knew was going to live forever.

Now he lives in mi heart.

IN MEMORY OF:
GURU "YORKY" OM

OCEANIACOM PRESS

Explore new horizons with us as we sail onto shores of latest products, events, great titles, and beyond.

Visit us:
www.oceaniacom.com

www.ingramcontent.com/pod-product-compliance
Lightning Source LLC
Chambersburg PA
CBHW011959090526
44590CB00023B/3781